Cambridge Elements

Elements in the History and Politics of Fascism
edited by
Federico Finchelstein
The New School for Social Research
António Costa Pinto
University of Lisbon

POPULISM AND FASCISM

Carlos de la Torre
University of Florida

Shaftesbury Road, Cambridge CB2 8EA, United Kingdom

One Liberty Plaza, 20th Floor, New York, NY 10006, USA

477 Williamstown Road, Port Melbourne, VIC 3207, Australia

314–321, 3rd Floor, Plot 3, Splendor Forum, Jasola District Centre, New Delhi – 110025, India

103 Penang Road, #05–06/07, Visioncrest Commercial, Singapore 238467

Cambridge University Press is part of Cambridge University Press & Assessment, a department of the University of Cambridge.

We share the University's mission to contribute to society through the pursuit of education, learning and research at the highest international levels of excellence.

www.cambridge.org
Information on this title: www.cambridge.org/9781009528993

DOI: 10.1017/9781009528979

© Carlos de la Torre 2025

This publication is in copyright. Subject to statutory exception and to the provisions of relevant collective licensing agreements, no reproduction of any part may take place without the written permission of Cambridge University Press & Assessment.

When citing this work, please include a reference to the DOI 10.1017/9781009528979

First published 2025

A catalogue record for this publication is available from the British Library

ISBN 978-1-009-52899-3 Hardback
ISBN 978-1-009-52898-6 Paperback
ISSN 2977–0416 (online)
ISSN 2977–0408 (print)

Cambridge University Press & Assessment has no responsibility for the persistence or accuracy of URLs for external or third-party internet websites referred to in this publication and does not guarantee that any content on such websites is, or will remain, accurate or appropriate.

For EU product safety concerns, contact us at Calle de José Abascal, 56, 1°, 28003 Madrid, Spain, or email eugpsr@cambridge.org.

Populism and Fascism

Elements in the History and Politics of Fascism

DOI: 10.1017/9781009528979
First published online: January 2025

Carlos de la Torre
University of Florida

Author for correspondence: Carlos de la Torre, delatorre.carlos@latam.ufl.edu

Abstract: The elections of Donald Trump and Jair Bolsonaro, as well as the strengthening of the radical right globally, brought back debates about the similarities and differences between populism and fascism. This Element argues that fascism and populism are similar insofar as they construct the people as one, understand leadership as embodiment, and perform politics of the extraordinary. They are different because there is a consensus that fascism occurred at a particular historical moment, and what came after was postfascism. There is not such an agreement to restrict populism to a historical moment. These isms also differ in the use of violence to deal with enemies, and in how they construct their legitimacy using elections or abolishing democracy. Whereas fascism destroys democracy and replaces elections with plebiscitary acclamation, populists promise to give power back to the people. Yet, when in power, the logic of populism leads to democratic erosion.

This Element also has a video abstract: www.cambridge.org/delatorre

Keywords: populism, fascism, charismatic leadership, violence, extraordinary politics

© Carlos de la Torre 2025

ISBNs: 9781009528993 (HB), 9781009528986 (PB), 9781009528979 (OC)
ISSNs: 2977-0416 (online), 2977-0408 (print)

Contents

Preface	1
1 Introduction: Fascism or Populism?	2
2 Defining and Explaining Fascism and Populism	11
3 Similarities	24
4 Differences	35
5 Fascism, Populism, and Democracy	46
6 Conclusions	56
References	60

Preface

The global strengthening of the populist radical right, which some prefer to categorize as wannabe fascist or postfascist, constitutes perhaps the major challenge to liberal democracy since its crises in the 1920s and 1930s that led to the establishment of fascist regimes or to the adoption of some of their practices and policies across the world. During the interwar period the left and the right proposed dictatorship as the alternative to the crises of parliamentary democracy. Fascism, as Finchelstein and Pinto have demonstrated, was a global phenomenon. Its appeal diminished significantly after the Axis Powers lost the war and the world was exposed to their genocide of populations racialized as inferior. Yet the specter of fascism never fully disappeared. Small, marginalized groups proudly labeled themselves fascists. In the last decades of the twentieth century and the beginning of the twenty-first century, radical right parties, many of them of fascist origins, became normalized and are attempting to win office or more likely to be part of coalition governments in Europe. Narendra Modi aims to rebuild a Hindu nation excluding its Muslim population, and Benjamin Netanyahu is attempting to replace a secular state, further marginalizing non-Jewish Israeli citizens and the Palestinian population. In the Americas a new type of right-wing leader like Donald Trump, Jair Bolsonaro, and Javier Milei has won elections. Once in office they delegitimized democratic institutions and thrived on polarization. Trump and Bolsonaro disregarded the basic democratic principle that elections are the only legitimate venue to get to power. When they lost the vote, they cried fraud and their followers led violent takeovers of Congress.

Are we experiencing the return of fascism? How best to characterize these leaders, their movements, and their enablers? Is a leader enough for fascism? Or are a party and movements in the streets needed to properly describe them as fascist? These are not only academic but also profoundly normative questions. Are we willing to give up on a democracy that is built on pluralism, that defends the rights of people to hold different beliefs, and in which dialogue is the tool used to convince rivals of one's arguments? Will notions of the heterosexual and patriarchal family replace the rights of citizens to choose their sexuality, and women's reproductive rights? Will nativism and xenophobia trump efforts to build multiethnic democracies?

To make sense of our turbulent times we need to base our speculations about the future "on an accurate analysis of the past" (Mosse 1999: 44). This is not the first comparison of fascism and populism (Berezin 2019; Eatwel 2017; Finchelstein 2017, 2024; Gentile 2024; Germani 1967, 1978; Hennessy 1976; Laclau 1977) nor a systematic review of the academic controversies around each of these concepts (de la Torre 2019; Kallis 2003; Pinto 1995). This Element provides a synthesis of the debates focusing on the different effects of fascism and populism on democracy. Their similarities and differences need to be clearly spelled out to assess the populists' claim that they improve democracy by returning power to the people, or the fascists' notion that plebiscitary acclamation and unity behind a larger-than-life leader express the popular will better than liberal representation.

This Element is intended for a general audience, undergraduate students, and specialists. It uses simple words to discuss theoretical, conceptual, and historical processes in a rigorous yet accessible way. It follows the steps of Latin American scholars who have compared these isms since Juan Perón was in office in the 1940s and 1950s. Gino Germani (1967) focused on their distinct class bases and their emergence under different moments of the modernization process. Ernesto Laclau (1977) argued that fascism is a populism of the dominant classes that emerged in a moment of crisis of the left and of the power bloc. For Federico Finchelstein (2014), populism is fascism adapted to democratic times when leaders and their movements renounced violently eliminating their enemies and accepted elections.

I have been working on populism, democratization, and authoritarianism since the 1990s. I started to compare populism with fascism when Nadia Urbinati and Federico Finchelstein invited me to present at the Fascism across Borders international conference at Columbia University and The New School for Social Research in 2015. This Element relies on and develops some of my previous arguments that despite their similarities populism and fascism are different isms (de la Torre 2022; de la Torre and Srisa-nga 2022). In my research I used historical-sociological and ethnographic approaches to theorize on the relationship of populism with democracy and authoritarianism. More recently I have immersed myself in the historical and theoretical literature on fascism to contrast it with populism. I have delivered papers on this Element's project in invited lectures at the University of Kiel, the University of Guadalajara, the Catholic University of Peru, and the Federal University of Ceará.

1 Introduction: Fascism or Populism?

The words *populism* and *fascism* are not confined to academic circles. These terms have left the ivory tower, becoming combat words widely used by politicians, pundits, and citizens to insult rivals or to try to come to terms with the unexpected political developments of the twenty-first century. Contrary to the predictions of most pundits, Donald Trump won the 2016 election; after he was defeated by Joe Biden, his followers organized a failed coup d'état. Despite four indictments, ninety-one felony charges, and convictions in thirty-four charges, Trump won the 2024 elections. His admirers Jair Bolsonaro and Javier Milei became the presidents of Brazil and Argentina, the two largest countries of South America. Bolsonaro followed Trump's playbook and his followers tried a failed coup when he lost the election to his archenemy, Lula da Silva of the leftist Workers Party, in 2022. Yet differently from Trump, Bolsonaro was prohibited by the superior electoral court from running for office until 2030. He was also accused of overseeing a broad conspiracy to hold on to power regardless of the results of the 2022 elections. Gone are the days in Europe when the traditional right and the center-left formed a cordon sanitaire to stop extremist radical right-wingers from winning elections or ruling as if they were normal parties.

How do we make sense of these conundrums? Are we experiencing a renaissance of fascism and a crisis of democracy like the experiences of the 1920s and 1930s? Or, alternatively, are these manifestations of populism in its radical right-wing variants? Does using the term *populism* absolve radical right parties of fascist origins like Georgia Meloni's Fratelli d' Italia of their past? Can the concept of populism be restricted to its right- or left-wing variants only? Are we living at the beginning of the twenty-first century under a new historical constellation that historian Enzo Traverso (2019) calls postfascism? Or are we seeing the emergence of what historian Federico Finchelstein (2024: 3) labels wannabe fascists that, at least for now, are "weaker and more incompetent than classical fascists"? What are the dangers of labeling leaders and movements that use elections and do not rely on paramilitary groups as fascists? Is this term further trivialized when used as an emotional weapon that could get in the way of rational debates?

These normative and theoretical questions are difficult indeed because the academic community has not agreed on how we define these categories. Scholars have defined populism and fascism as ideologies, strategies, and styles to get to power and to govern, and as regimes. For some, fascism is a type of populism of the ruling classes (Laclau 1977). For others, Nazism and fascism have a populist phase before they become regimes. Historian Peter Fritzche (2016: 5) wrote, "the idea of 'the people' was both the rhetorical ground on which National Socialists operated and the horizon for which they reached." Others see a danger in the overextension of these concepts. Some propose that scholars stop using fascism (Allayrdyce 2003); others argue that populism has been robbed "of its specific historical content . . . At this point the concept of populism loses much, if not all, of its validity as a transnational analytical category" (Jones 2016: 33).

If scholars cannot agree on what fascism and populism are and if they are even valuable and useful concepts, how to stop the proliferation of abuses of these terms by pundits, citizens, and politicians who use them to label whoever they dislike? *Populism* is used to categorize politicians and their followers as irrational, the poorly educated who respond with their guts instead of their brains. Yet not all consider that this word is a stigma. Jean-Luc Mélenchon, leader of La France Insoumise, for example, uses it as a badge of honor because he says he is against elites. Differently from leaders in other world regions, right-wing and other politicians in the United States dispute who is the authentic populist. Criticizing candidate Donald Trump, President Barack Obama called himself populist. After winning the 2016 election Steve Bannon, MAGA strategist and ideologue, asserted, "Trump is the leader of a populist uprising" (de la Torre and Srisa-nga 2022: 2). Differently from the 1920s and 1930s when elites, social scientists, artists, and intellectuals proudly collaborated with and belonged to fascist parties and movements, nowadays very few people use the term as a self-definition. It is more often a stigma and a reminder that fascism caused the death of about 40 million civilians and 20 million soldiers during the Second World War.[1] Does this mean that fascism was just the product of a particular historical constellation, and if so, was it a unique phenomenon? Or can fascism manifest itself differently under new historical conjunctures?

This Element analyzes how scholars have used these concepts, their similarities, and their differences, and how they undermined or replaced democracy with one-person dictatorships conceptualized as lasting over time. But before proceeding, it is worthwhile describing the socioeconomic and political transformations that led to the emergence and normalization of the radical right in Europe and the Americas in the twenty-first century.

Europe

A good place to start is Cas Mudde's description of the mainstreaming of the far right illustrated by the different actions of citizens, the media, and European institutions when the Austrian Freedom Party (FPÖ) was invited to join coalition governments in 2000 and again eighteen years later.

> In 2000, the FPÖ entered a coalition government with the conservative Austrian People's Party, which led to massive pushback in Austria and Europe. Egged on by the Austrian Social Democrats, which had negotiated in secret with FPÖ too, hundreds of thousands of Austrians took to the streets to demonstrate against the "fascist" government. The (then) fourteen other EU member states had tried to prevent the coalition with a strong statement, saying they would "not promote or accept any bilateral official contacts at a political level" with a government including the FPÖ. In the end, the EU-14 only boycotted the FPÖ ministers and appointed a committee of three "wise men," which recommended that the sanctions should be lifted. Despite

---

[1] https://news.un.org/en/story/2021/05/1091582.

> mutterings from some EU member states, and the Austrian Social Democrats, the sanctions were lifted after less than a year.
> When the FPÖ returned to government in 2018, there were much smaller demonstrations in Austria, and no EU government boycotted FPÖ ministers. (Mudde 2019: 49)

One might be tempted to conclude that the FPÖ and other radical right parties have moderated their ideologies and proposals, but, as Mudde shows, that was not the case. After the Great Recession of 2008, terrorist attacks in Europe, and the 2017 refugee crisis, the traditional right and some social democrats have increasingly accepted the radical right discourse on immigration, law and order, European integration, and corruption. The media has become supportive of radical right politicians and parties as well, and the social web has allowed for the proliferation of extreme right-wing subcultures.

The strengthening of the radical right is also a result of how democratization was designed in the postwar era to constrain popular sovereignty. The goal was to exorcise the ghosts of fascism and communism, whose roots allegedly laid in appeals to popular sovereignty and to "the people" by strengthening constitutional courts and safeguarding individual rights. Jan-Werner Müller (2011: 150) argues that a constrained form of democracy was created in which politics "was not supposed to be a source of meaning." László Sólyom, president of the Hungarian Constitutional Court from 1990 to 1998 and president of Hungary from 2005 to 2010, explained:

> The new constitutional courts were created out of a deep mistrust for the majoritarian institutions, which had been misused and corrupted in the Fascist and Communist regimes. In this given historical setting, the constitutional courts believed they represented the essence of the democratic change and enjoyed "revolutionary legitimacy." Little wonder if some constitutional courts have been inclined to replace the motto "we the people" with "we the court." (Furedi 2018: 192)

Appeals to popular sovereignty could not be buried by design in a democracy. The FPÖ, the French National Front, and other European right-wing parties first; later the movements of the squares of "the indignant" in Spain, Greece, and elsewhere; and subsequently parties of the left like Syriza, Podemos, and La France Insoumise challenged the loss of national sovereignty to supranational organizations, and the surrender of popular sovereignty to elites. Social democrats have accepted neoliberalism with the argument that there are no alternatives, and as a result politics "has become a mere issue of managing the established order, a domain reserved for experts, and popular sovereignty has been declared obsolete" (Mouffe 2018: 17). Neoliberalism and globalization led to the decline of working-class organizations, as well as of social democrats and other parties of the left, and to the erosion of class identities. Appeals to the heterogenous people replaced appeals to class. Yet the vague category of the people was imagined differently by the left, which constructed it as the plebs – those excluded from political and economic power by elites – and the right, which used cultural, religious, and ethnic criteria to imagine the people as an ethnos (Roberts 2023).

The United States

Differently from the recent past when two pragmatic parties sought the support of swing voters who recognized the legitimacy of their rivals, entered into agreements with them, and accepted the results of elections to peacefully transfer power, currently the US is polarized. Whereas the Republican Party has become a white Christian party in the hands of extreme right activists and leaders, the Democratic Party is multiracial and more secular. Left-wing, center, and right-wing politicians and activists coexist inside the Democratic Party tent. The roots of US polarization were the successful demands of the social movements of the 1960s that democratized American culture and identity. Whereas the Democratic Party became the umbrella for activists for racial, gender, and sexual equality, the Republican Party was at the forefront of resistance to the rights to abortion, same-sex marriage, and racial equality. Political parties became ideologically polarized around race, religion, geography, cultural issues, and even "ways of life" (Levitsky and Ziblatt 2018: 167). Society thus split up in cultural wars between secular and liberal understandings of the body, sexuality, and identity, and religious-traditionalist views of the family and sexual differences between men and women. Polarization is even manifested in marriage decisions. In 1960 about 4 percent of Americans said they would be displeased if their child married someone from the other party; by 2020 that number grew to about 40 percent.[2]

As in Europe, neoliberal globalization resulted in the bifurcation of the job market between a few well-paid jobs and low-paid service jobs that did not offer opportunities for social mobility. The end of well-paid unionized factory jobs led to a "sense of economic irrelevance, dislocation and declining material and occupational security" (Cohen 2019: 9). The logic of producerism was used to differentiate manly white workers, who provide for their families, live off of the products of their labor, and pay taxes, from parasites of color, who allegedly do not work and make a living from government handouts. Whereas the Populist Party in the late nineteenth century branded financial elites as bloodsuckers who live off of the hard work of manual workers, since the 1960s African Americans, other people of color, immigrants, intellectuals, and state officials who do not

---

[2] www.nytimes.com/2024/01/25/us/politics/biden-trump-presidential-election.html.

make tangible objects became labeled freeloaders who live off of the hard work and taxes paid by white producers. The extreme right claimed that producers were also abused by liberal anti-family policies that fomented the perversion of Christian values by recognizing abortion, same-sex marriage, and LGTBQ rights. The Tea Party during Obama's administration and later Donald Trump used these discursive representations to claim to stand for the interests of white producers and for defending the family from perverts' attacks.

After four years in office Trump was able to transform the Republican Party into his own MAGA party, but, alas, he was unable to destroy democracy. He profited from deepening the polarization between white and Christian real Americans of all social classes and educational levels. Trump and his enablers in the Republican Party, Fox News, and some religious leaders raised the stakes of elections, pitching them as existential battles where the survival of an ethnic and religious group was at stake. When Trump and some Republicans refused to accept that they lost an election and claimed that they would only accept results that favored them, they put in doubt the fundamental principle of democratic alternation. After Trump supporters violently took over Congress, and many Republican legislators continued to be loyal to him, did they abandon democracy? If Trump, his enablers, and followers are fascists, why did they use elections to get to power in 2024? Is their project to protect the privileges of white citizens, restricting democracy and transforming it into what O'Donnell and Schmitter (1986: 13) defined as a limited political democracy, a "democradura," or as a soft dictatorship "dictablanda"?

Latin America

The radical right arrived in Latin America, probably to stay. Bolsonaro won the Brazilian elections against the leftist Workers Party in 2018. José Antonio Kats formed the Republican Party as an alternative to the traditional right that had accepted the welfare state and promoted same-sex marriage and was defeated in a runoff election by leftist Gabriel Boric in 2021 in Chile. Libertarian and anti-gender-ideology candidate Javier Milei won the 2023 elections in Argentina. This is not the first antiestablishment right-wing populist wave in Latin America. Neoliberal populists emerged in the 1990s against traditional parties, promising the reduction of the state, self-regulation of the economy, globalization, and law and order.

Alberto Fujimori arose in a context of hyperinflation, when two guerrilla groups were on the verge of taking over the Peruvian state. He ruled for ten years, curbed hyperinflation, delivered "order and security" by defeating the guerrillas and arresting the leader of the Shining Path, and, with the excuse of ending terrorism, abused human rights, especially of peasant and Indigenous people. In 1992 he achieved a self-coup, closed Congress, and enacted a new constitution (McClintok 2013).

Álvaro Uribe was president of Colombia between 2002 and 2010. He emerged in a context of a deep security crises (Bejarano 2013: 328). His law-and-order approach reduced crime rates and brought security at the cost of human rights abuses and the concentration of power in his hands.

Nayib Bukele promised law and order to control the power of gangs that had become a parallel state in some communities in El Salvador (Wolf 2021: 67). His administration incarcerated without a proper trial and abused the human rights of about 71,000 people in a population of 6.5 million. As the homicide and crime rates diminished, Bukele's popularity increased. After reforming the constitution, which forbade reelection, he won an overwhelming majority of votes in 2024.

The novelty of radical right politicians such as Bolsonaro, Milei, and Kats is that in addition to favoring neoliberalism and law and order, they emerged as a backlash to women's rights, LGTBQ+ rights, and the empowerment of non-whites. Their pro-family and morality proposals resonated with a conservative Christian base made up of evangelicals, Pentecostals, and right-wing Catholics. Sectors of the middle class felt threatened by the empowerment and social mobility of nonwhites in Brazil (Porto 2023). Kats, following Trump, vowed to construct walls on the borders with Peru and Bolivia (Rovira Kaltwasser 2019: 49). He also promised to militarize territories where the Indigenous Mapuche people were resisting timber exploitation, labeling Indigenous activists terrorists (53). Milei is a libertarian who promised to shrink the state so as to let the market regulate itself. He opposed LQTBQ+, women, and Indigenous rights.

Even though Bolsonaro failed as a president, mainly due to his denial of Covid, which resulted in thousands of unnecessary deaths, and he is currently banned from running for office, the movement that supported him remains strong. The number of Brazilians who consider themselves on the right jumped from 20 percent in 2020 to 40 percent in 2021 (Avritzer and Renno 2023: 256). Bolsonarism is made up of groups

> that mobilize mainly on social networks around certain key ideas including the perception of a common enemy (the left, in general, and the Partido dos Trabalhadores [Workers' Party – PT], in particular), moral conservatism (defense of the traditional family, patriarchy, and a Christian nation), economic liberalism (neoliberalism, the theology of prosperity, the inviolability of private property, and entrepreneurship), patriotism (Brazil above everything), and public safety (as in the saying that the only good criminal is a dead criminal). (Bernardino Costa 2023: 99)

Democratic institutions, a strong civil society, and the private media constrained Bolsonaro. His administration disrupted environmental, human rights, educational, and health state policies established by center and left parties in the previous decades. His rhetoric against Indigenous people, environmentalists, feminists, anti-racist activists, and LGTBQ+ groups resulted in the assassination of Indigenous activists, the further destruction of the Amazon rainforest, increasing violent attacks on transgender citizens, and aggressive and vulgar attacks on feminists and anti-racist activists. But democracy and even some policies challenged by Bolsonaro like class and racial quotas for higher education survived. Bolsonarism as a movement was not defeated, and new leaders could probably emerge.

Conclusion and Questions to Be Addressed in Future Sections

I use the term *radical right* to characterize movements, parties, and governments in Europe and the Americas. This term has been employed descriptively, and in the following sections the definitions of *fascism*, *right-wing populism*, *postfascism*, and *wannabe fascists* will be analyzed in detail. The debates on how to characterize these families of right-wing politics are important for several reasons.

First, because whereas historical fascism got rid of democracy, replacing it with rituals of plebiscitary acclamation, populist legitimacy lies in wining free and open elections. Thus, populists limited but did not abolish rights of free information and organization.

Second, whereas it is relatively easy to point to the actions and the date when democracy was abolished by fascists in Italy, Spain, or Germany, it is very difficult to recognize the slow processes of democratic erosion under populism. When in office populists concentrate power in the hands of the president, reducing the clout of legislatures, and the judicial system is put in the hands of loyal followers who use it to punish critics with the appearance of following legality. The private media is censored and intimidated, but not abolished. Parallel organizations are created in civil society to diminish the power of independent social movements and nongovernmental organizations.

Third, there is a scholars' agreement that classical fascism was the result of a coalescence of historical forces such as the banalization of death after the First World War, the fear of the diffusion of Bolshevism, the crises of democracy, the appeal of dictatorship for the right and the left, and the Great Depression. Whatever came after is called postfacism (Griffin 2020; Traverso 2019).

Populism is not confined to a historical period and has emerged in societies with different levels of democratization and modernization, as well as in the

Global South and Global North. Differently from fascism, populism can be from the right when the people are built as an ethnos, or from the left when they are constructed as the plebs. Finally, the terms *populism* and *fascism* simultaneously illuminate and obscure. *Populism*, for instance, could be used to absolve right-wing parties from their fascist past, or to blame their authoritarianism on their nativism (Mudde and Rovira Kaltwasser 2017: 83). If elections are used to legitimately get to power, populists belong to the democratic and not the fascist camp. But how to interpret the actions of self-described democrats who do not accept losing elections because they think of themselves as the only legitimate candidate of the true people? Are they fascist when they organize rebellions, plot military coups, or delegitimize elections? Can fascism be reduced to the actions of leaders, or do they need fascist parties, paramilitary organizations, and a mass movement in the streets as well? Are Trump and Bolsonaro wannabe fascists who were not able to get rid of democracy because of their lack of will and strategy, or due to the resistance of institutions, state officials, social movements, and the media?

This Element selectively uses some of the enormous historical and social scientific literature on fascism and populism to compare their similarities and especially to point out their differences. The sections distinguish the dynamics of these isms, differentiating when they were movements challenging the power of elites, when they got to office, and the institutional and structural conditions that allowed them to establish new regimes. It looks at the historicity of fascism and populism and their interactions with their allies, enablers, and enemies. It focuses on cases that the literature does not doubt to name fascist or populists even though some scholars challenge the inclusion of Nazism as fascism, and others question the validity of putting leaders with radically different economic policies such as Perón, Chávez, Trump, or Bolsonaro in the same analytical basket.

Section 2 focuses on the epistemological and conceptual strategies of different attempts to define fascism and populism. The selection of theoretical and conceptual approaches is not exhaustive and reviews cumulative, minimum, and complex definitions. It advocates for the latter because it takes ideologies, organizations, performances, and styles of communication into account. Complex definitions allow focusing on gradations to differentiate light from full-blown cases. For instance, different from politicians who might occasionally use populist tropes, styles of communication, and performances, others perform populism most of the time. Complex definitions also allow us to explore when fascism became populism and where it is mutating back to fascism or postfascism in the twenty-first century.

Section 3 shows the similarities of fascism and populism when contrasted with liberal-democratic logic and its key ideas and practices. It explores their construction of the category of the people, their notion of leadership, and their performance of politics of the extraordinary in mass events, meetings, and demonstrations.

Section 4 argues that despite the similarities discussed previously, populism and fascism are distinct because of how they use and perform violence, their legitimation strategies, and their historicity. Whereas populism has occurred at different historical times and in distinct geographical regions, under diverse moments of modernization and democratization, fascism was the product of a particular historical constellation, and whatever came after that was postfascism. Yet when right-wing populists like Trump and Bolsonaro do not accept elections and instigate followers to use physical violence, what are they?

Fascist and populist relations to democracy are explored in Section 5. After fascists were invited to govern by traditional elites, they outmaneuvered other conservative forces. They got rid of democracy yet preserved elites' economic power and status. Populists, despite their claims to be democratic innovators who promise to give power back to the people, brought democratic decay, and in some historical and institutional circumstances forged populist hybrid regimes that either democratized or moved to became full dictatorships. Section 5 focuses on the interactions between political actors under different institutional, historical, and structural constellations. It shows the possible outcomes of these confrontations and argues that, nowadays and for the time being, wannabe fascists or right-wing radical populists have not been able to destroy democracy and replace it with dictatorship. Rather, while in office, they further delegitimize institutions and procedures. Fascists replace democracy with one-person dictatorships that allegedly express the popular will better than elections. They imagine fascist dictatorships as long-lasting. As long as populists use elections as the legitimate tool to get to office, they remain in the democratic camp. Yet they contribute to further move democracies in crises to the grayer area between autocracy and democracy. Whereas some democratize, others move to full dictatorship.

2 Defining and Explaining Fascism and Populism

This section analyzes the different epistemological and conceptual strategies used to define these isms. It starts with Gino Germani's pioneering differentiation of fascism and national populism in terms of their class base and emergence at distinct periods of modernization. Then it explores arguments to get rid of these ambiguous concepts in the social sciences, or to preserve them just as insults. Subsequently it focuses on minimum and concise definitions that could be used to compare cases in different historical times and geographical spaces.

Minimum definitions have been criticized because they are reductionist. As an alternative, scholars have created complex definitions to make sense of gradations and to preserve the thickness of social reality. The challenge is to produce complex concepts that could be useful for comparative research, avoiding such a long list of traits that confines the category to fit just one or two cases.

Modernization, Mass Society, and Social Class

Italian-Argentinean sociologist Gino Germani was the first scholar who systematically compared fascism and national populism. In the introduction to his volume *Authoritarianism, Fascism, and National Populism* he explains the personal reasons that motivated his lifetime scholarly endeavor.

> I was a child when fascism reached power in Italy, and still a teenager when it established a totalitarian state. In my early youth I experienced the total ideological climate involving the everyday life of the common citizen, and more strongly so, the younger generation. Later in Argentina, where I went as a political refugee, I met another variety of authoritarianism. Both Italian fascism and Argentinean Peronism came to power as an outcome of the crises of liberal-democratic regimes hitherto considered fairly well established. (Germani 1978: vii)

Germani was arrested by Mussolini's police when he was a young antifascist activist, and as an adult he temporarily lost his job as a college professor under Peronism. It is worth remembering that General Juan Perón started his political life in 1943 as a member of a pro-Axis military junta. Among other positions he served as the secretary of labor, and in this role he jailed or co-opted labor leaders while promoting collective bargaining agreements, increasing wages, delivering paid vacations to workers, and raising their social status. Perón was arrested by his fellow junta members in October 1945 because of his prolabor policies but was rescued a few days later by labor demonstrations that demanded his liberation. He abandoned fascism after his release, won the free and open elections of 1946, and served two terms until he was deposed by a military coup in 1954. Despise dropping fascism and wining free elections, he continued to be labeled a dictator by many foreign commentators, perhaps because he closed newspapers and repressed the opposition.

Differently from his contemporaries who considered Perón a fascist, Germani used the dominant sociological paradigms of his time – modernization and mass society theory – to explore the similarities and differences between fascism and national populism. His model of change is based on the notion of social integration. He explained,

> [A] society is integrated if there exists sufficient correspondence between three levels: the normative level (the institutionalized and legitimate norms, values, statuses, and roles regulating social actions); the psychosocial level (the internalization of the norms, values, etc., in terms of motivations, attitudes, aspirations, and character structure); and the environmental level (the whole external context within which social actions take place). When such correspondence exists, individual behavior will be precisely that predicted by the normative structure. It will be institutionalized and legitimated behavior. (Germani 1967: 193)

Abrupt social change such as rapid urbanization, industrialization, or dislocation due to disaster or war produces breakdown or disintegration that could lead to anomie, meaning that actors do not have a normative structure to make sense of the new social conditions and then to act rationally. During crises of normative integration and anomie actors follow their emotions, acting irrationally, and could be mobilized. Germani distinguishes primary mobilization that occurred in the transition from a traditional to a modern society and when actors were excluded from the political community, from secondary mobilization in partially modernized and democratized societies. Whereas Italian fascism was a process of secondary mobilization caused by the upheavals of the First World War and the Russian Revolution, Peronism was a primary mobilization of actors previously left out of the political system. The class base of these movements was different as well. The social base of Perón's national populism was recent internal migrants from the countryside to the cities not previously socialized into working-class cultures. Because they were in a state of anomie, they responded to the emotional appeals of Perón and his wife, Eva, obtaining material as well as symbolic rewards. The downwardly mobile middle class was the social base of Italian fascism that only got ersatz satisfaction in the forms of imperialism and racism.

Germani considers national populism as a sui generis type of authoritarianism, similar yet fundamentally different from fascism because of the social conditions under which national populism and fascism emerged and their class bases. He links national populism to the transition to modernity and to the incorporation of previously excluded masses. Yet populist movements, parties, leaders, and governments have emerged under different social conditions and in nations with dissimilar levels of modernization and democratization. His distinction between these isms could be maintained only if populism is linked exclusively, as Germani did, to the transition to modernity and the term *fascism* is used to describe leaders, parties, and movements in partially modernized and democratized societies. This model could perhaps explain the differences between what Latin Americanist scholars call classical populism of leaders such as Perón, and the radical populist right. Thus Donald Trump or Jair Bolsonaro could be characterized as fascist instead of right-wing populist. But what to do with self-described leftists such as Hugo Chávez in Venezuela or Rafael Correa in Ecuador, whose policies were nationalist, statist, redistributive, and anti-imperialist? These politicians were certainly authoritarian in how they constructed and dealt with enemies, but they were poles apart from fascism unless this term is used as synonymous with any type of autocratic government.

A second empirical problem is that social class alone does not explain the appeal of these isms. The new working class in a state of anomie that Germani put at the center of his interpretation, as well as the older working class that was socialized by anarchists, communists, and socialists supported Perón because they had obtained material and symbolic rewards when he was the secretary of labor. Mussolini and other fascists were backed not only by the middle class. They "drew support from all classes" (Mann 2004: 20). Ian Kershaw (2015: 231) agrees when he writes fascism cannot be defined "as simply a middle-class movement, or, indeed, in unequivocal class terms at all." Class is important to explain these isms, if instead of trying to attach a movement to a particular class, we focus on historical processes of class formation. Whereas in advanced capitalist nations class was a major cleavage and source of political and social identity, in most nations of the Global South social heterogeneity and class fragmentation were articulated in cleavages around the populist notion of the people against the elites instead of class. With the changes in the social structure of the Global North that reduced class salience and identities, the populist opposition to the elites is becoming a new cleavage that perhaps is replacing class (Roberts 2023).

Like other structuralist class theories, Germani ignores populists' or fascists' own beliefs. Even though there was an attempt to include emotions and reasons, the first were reduced to irrational responses of masses in a state of anomie. Scores of social historians and sociologists have shown that organization and political opportunity explain protest better than anomie and breakdown.

Fascism and populism should be banned from academia but perhaps retained as insults. Because fascism has been used to characterize such a dissimilar range of movements, parties, and leaders in several world regions and historical times, critics, with good reason, have argued that it has suffered from semantic inflation. Some scholars have proposed to get rid of this concept. Historian Stuart Wolf in 1968 wrote, "Perhaps the word fascism should be banned, at least temporarily from our political vocabulary" (Griffin 2020: 39). Historian Gilbert Allardyce (2003: 51) emphatically noted, "There is no such thing as fascism. There are only men and movements that we call by that name." He concluded, "Full of emotion and empty of real meaning, the word fascism is one of the most abused and abusive in our political vocabulary" (54).

Similarly, scholars of populism periodically propose to ban this term because it is used indiscriminately to refer to right and leftist politicians who pursued neoliberal or statist policies. Political theorist Benjamín Arditti (2024), well known for his analysis of populism and democracy, proposes to move our conversation from the question "What is populism?" to "Is there such a thing as populism?" He offers three responses that he calls provocations. The first is to get rid of populism as a category of the social sciences because populism does not exist. He writes, "Populism as we know has passed its sell-by date and can be dropped, just as we have stopped asking whether monarchs have a divine right to rule." If the academic community insists on continuing to use populism, they should keep it as an insult or restrict the term to analyzing a particular historical moment. His second provocation to reduce populism to an insult will not allow researchers to explain the ambiguities of populist challenges to real, existing democracies. Populists point to problems that other politicians tried to ignore, yet their solutions undermine democratic conviviality and pluralism. It is important to differentiate between types of populism. Some are exclusionary of the other built with religious, ethnic, and racial criteria while other populists seek to include the politically, culturally, and socioeconomically marginalized sectors of society. Arditti's third solution is perhaps the most problematic because if scholars of populism agree on something, it is to not restrict populism to one moment in history.

Despite the attempt to ban these categories from academia, these concepts will probably stay with us for good. Hence following the spirit of their abolitionist critics, we should not use these categories for empirical research without first reflecting on their epistemological and theoretical assumptions. In what follows the epistemological and conceptual strategies of scholars who advocate for minimum definitions are contrasted with complex constructs that aim to be open to ambiguities and gradations.

Minimum Definitions

Some scholars consider that fascism and populism are phenomena and realities of the social world. To understand and explain observable facts, they have developed minimal definitions that clearly differentiate their object of study from other phenomena. Their goal is to avoid fuzziness, developing elegant and parsimonious short definitions that can travel across time and space. First, they must identify the domain of reality where their object of study can be clearly located, such as ideology, the economy, politics, etcetera. Influenced by Michael Frieden's concept of ideology, they have distinguished its core from adjacent or peripheral components.

Roger Griffin built on fascist self-interpretations to construct a minimum ideological definition of generic fascism in order to differentiate it from other forms of authoritarianism. He defined fascism as "a genus of political ideology whose mythic core in its various permutations is a palingenetic form of populist ultranationalism" (Griffin 2008: 88–89). The ultranation is an imagined community that "like a living organism, can decline and 'die,' or regenerate itself and return to enough strength culturally and politically to realize renewed greatness inspired by past glories" (Griffin 2020: 83). Palingenesis is the myth of rebirth from decadence "to be realized by removing obstacles to or 'enemies' of the nation's renewal" (83). Fascism at its core is a hybrid of these two "mythic elements: the myth of rebirth or palingenesis, and the myth of the organic nation or race, the 'ultranation'" (90). Even though Griffin wrote that populism should be clearly distinguished from fascism, his definition of fascism casts it as "populist ultranationalism." The adjacent element of fascism is the creation of a pervasive populist movement "to mobilize and unleash the dormant power of 'the people' to cleanse itself from the forces of decadence and regenerate itself in a new era of greatness" (92).

Cas Mudde also used Michael Freeden to define populism as a thin ideology linked to thick ideologies such as conservatism or socialism. He defines populism as "an ideology that considers society to be ultimately separated into two homogeneous and antagonistic groups, 'the pure people' versus 'the corrupt elite,' and which argues that politics should be an expression of the *volonté générale* (general will) of the people" (Mudde 2004: 543). With his coauthor Cristóbal Rovira Kaltwasser, in a later publication he wrote, "Populism is in essence a form of moral politics, as the distinction between 'the elite' and 'the people' is first and foremost moral (i.e. pure vs. corrupt), not situational (e.g. position of power), socio-cultural (e.g. ethnicity, religion), or socioeconomic (e.g. class)" (Mudde and Rovira Kaltwasser 2012: 8–9). Accordingly, populists construct politics as a Manichaean struggle between the forces of good and evil.

Federico Finchelstein (2017: 54) argues that the search for a minimum definition resembles looking for the fascist or populist "Holy Grail." While elegant and parsimonious, minimum ideological definitions reduce the complexity of these isms to one of their fundamental components. These ideological definitions are silent on party organizations, communication styles, or charismatic leadership, for example. Minimalist definitions put aside traits or components labeled as peripheral or adjacent and not core to their theorization. For instance, the ideational definition of populism considers leadership as not central, thus imposing as universal a trait that works well for European radical right parties but does not explain these phenomena in the Global South, where populisms are leader centric. A fundamental problem of ideological definitions is that they do not explain who the carrier of the ideology is. It could be the population at large, a leader, a movement, or a political party. They assume that those who belonged to fascist or populist movements were just fascist or populist all the time. They do not differentiate between different levels of commitment, nor people's life histories and how they negotiated their different identities (Passamore 2014: 18).

Ideological minimum definitions sanitize these isms. Griffin cleans fascism of its violence, while other scholars (Finchelstein 2017; Kershaw 2015; Mann 2004; Traverso 2019) put violence as one of its definitional features. Similarly, Mudde and Rovira Kaltwatzer (2017: 83) absolve populism of authoritarianism when they argue that nativism and not populism is at the root of populism's exclusionary ideas assuming clear-cut separations between populist and nationalist appeals. Mudde and Rovira Kaltwasser (99) also normalized authoritarian populism when they wrote that "there is a dormant Hugo Chávez or Sarah Palin inside all of us." Finally, in their zeal to give the impression that there is a consensus around their classifications, some promoters of minimal definitions include authors who understand ideology differently. Griffin argues that Roger Eatwell (2017) shares his minimal definition when the latter includes violence and politics as well. Hawkins and Rovira Kaltwasser (2017) include scholars who use discourse analysis inspired by Ernesto Laclau as sharing in their discursive ideational definition.

From a Minimal Sartorian Definition to a Fuzzy Concept

Kurt Weyland (2001) in a very influential article redefined populism as a political strategy to get to power and to govern. His minimal definition locates populism in the political domain and considers that leaders appeal directly to their constituencies, bypassing traditional mediating institutions like parties and unions. The opposite of populism, he argued, is Weberian formal organizations and political parties. Because their main goal is to get to power and to stay, populists are opportunistic and pragmatic. Differently from zealous fascists, populists lack ideological commitments (Weyland 2019: 50). In a later publication, Weyland acknowledged that Sartorian definitional minimalism is not effective in differentiating populism from surrounding concepts. He reconceptualized populism as a fuzzy concept, meaning that it is not always easy to clearly differentiate populism from alternatives. Differently from the Sartorian goal to clearly distinguish a cat from a dog, populism might be a cat-dog because "in their quest for power leaders flexibly adjust to contextual opportunities and constrains and change color with the circumstances" (Weyland 2017a: 65).

Some leaders the literature does not label populist, at times and under certain circumstances, might use populist tropes. Under conditions of what Bernard Manin (1997) called audience democracies, when the personal qualities of the leader are more important than clear ideologies and politicians try to communicate directly with the electorate, we could expect that politicians might occasionally use populist rhetoric. Differently from leaders who occasionally use or perform populism, full-blown populists consistently perform populist styles, use a rhetoric of the antagonistic confrontation of the people against elites, and seek to communicate directly with electors using the media and mass meetings. Donald Trump, Hugo Chávez, and Juan Perón are good examples of full-blown populists, whereas light populists occasionally and selectively borrow from the populist discursive and performative playbooks.

Kevin Passmore (2014: 14) writes that a major problem with some theories of fascism and, I will add, of populism "is that they presume an undifferentiated and ultimately passive mass, integrated into fascism by ritual repetition of ideas and/or by technologies of rule." Some scholars of fascism do not pay attention to the different levels of involvement with and commitment of common people or followers to fascism. Whereas some, especially those who actively participated in paramilitary groups and organizations that required a high level of involvement, perhaps were true believers and acted as convinced fascists, others paid lip service to fascist ideologies or changed their loyalty over time (52, 65).

It is worth remembering that because fascists came to power after periods of brutal violence in Italy, or that in Germany the Nazis became ferociously repressive in office, people often "bow their heads in mock mental obeisance but refuse to internalize the system" (Baehr 2008: 49). Similarly, whereas poor people who often interact with party brokers accept the self-interpretations of populist politicians as protectors of the poor, those who sporadically interact with party brokers are not committed to the populist worldview nor to their party identities (Auyero 2001).

If common people varied in their allegiance to, commitment to, and belief in fascism, some leaders strategically shifted in and out of fascism, or adapted and drew inspirations from selective institutions. Antonio Salazar's "New State," the longest-lasting dictatorship in modern Europe, remained in power for thirty-six years, avoiding the "most aggressive and radical aspects of fascism, while integrating and deriving inspiration from some of the institutions derived from it" (Pinto 1995: v). Salazar did not create "a strong single party that held the monopoly on ideology, propaganda and the organization of the masses, the Portuguese New State did not codify the 'cult of the leader'" (Pinto 2007: 75). Yet a personality cult was created, and Salazar was built by state propaganda into a charismatic leader of similar stature as his neighbor Francisco Franco. In his earlier years Franco was para-fascist, anticommunist, and pro-Axis. In 1937 he merged the fascist Falange party with the Carlist monarchists, "altering its name to the most complex and absurd of all the fascist-type movements – Falange Española Tradicionalista y de las Juntas de Ofensiva Nacional-Sindicalista (FET-JONS)" (Payne 2007: 58). Later Spain mutated to "an inward looking, highly reactionary and illiberal Catholic state led by a personal dictator" (Griffin 2020: 132).

To make sense of the complexity of these isms and their transformations over time, more comprehensive definitions that look at their ideologies, organizations, and communication styles are needed. Complex definitions pay attention to gradations and to the fuzziness of these isms.

Complex Definitions

If one-sentence definitions are reductionist as they trim down complexity by focusing on just one aspect of the phenomena, the challenge is to avoid listing such large numbers of components that definitions become useful for a single historical experience only. This section draws on scholars who have developed complex definitions that consider ideologies, organizations, performances, and communication styles (Diehl 2024).

Ideologies

Differently from other ideologies such as liberalism or communism, fascism and populism have no sacred texts. Yet fascism and populism were major ideological innovations for their "capacity to fuse ideas and sentiments to create new public justifications for the exercise of power" (Müller 2011: 92). Whereas the Nazis were ideological fanatics, other fascists and populists were more pragmatic. Fascists were "ultranationalist, antiliberal, and anti-Marxist" (Finchelstein 2017: 15). They believed in an "organic" or "integral" nation, and this involved an unusually strong sense of the nation's "enemies," both abroad and (especially) at home (Mann 2004: 13). Because opponents were seen as enemies, they were to be removed and the nation cleansed of them (16). The enemy was constructed as "an existential threat to the nation and to its people that had to be first persecuted and then deported or eliminated" (Finchelstein 2017: 15).

Differently from conservatives who considered that the existing social order is essentially harmonious, fascists proposed to create a new order using the power of the state. They aimed to forge a totalitarian state in which plurality and civil society would be silenced, and there would increasingly be no distinctions between the public and the private, and between the state and its citizens ... [They] defended a divine, messianic, and charismatic form of leadership that conceived of the leader as organically linked to the people and the nation. It considered popular sovereignty to be fully delegated to the dictator, who acted in the name of the community of the people and knew better than they what they truly wanted. Fascists replaced history and empirically based notions of truth with political myth. (Finchelstein 2017: 15)

Populist ideology shared the fascist distinction between friend and enemy but without advocating for their physical elimination, and "a charismatic understanding of the leader as an embodiment of the voice and desires of the people and the nation as a whole" (Finchelstein 2017: 20). It invoked the people "in a two-fold opposition, at once vertical and horizontal, against 'those on top' (and sometimes also 'those on the bottom') on the one hand, and against an alien or threatening 'outside' on the other, generally in such a way that economic, political and cultural elites are represented as being 'outside' – or at least different or 'other' – as well as 'on top'" (Brubaker 2020: 60). Populist ideologies did not advocate for dictatorship; on the contrary, the only way for them to get legitimately to power is to win clean and competitive elections.

Organizations

When fascism emerged in Italy and Germany, most political parties were made up of notables who reached out to the public only during election times. Another characteristic was that they were class parties. Fascists innovated by appealing to all social classes and were successful in their recruitment efforts. Fascists engaged "committed militants rather than careerist politicians" (Paxton 2005: 58). They mobilized "the masses, giving them the illusion of being actors, not simple spectators of politics" (Traverso 2019: 105).

Michael Mann (2004: 16) writes that paramilitarism was both a key value and a quintessential organizational form of fascism, and that violence explains its radicalism. Fascists created a new type of party, the fascist militia party, which "operated in political struggles with warlike methods and considered political adversaries as 'internal enemies' that must be defeated and destroyed" (Gentile 2008: 292). Fascists had an all-encompassing conception of politics that subordinated "privacy-based values (religion, culture, morality, love etc.) to the preeminent political power" (297). Paramilitary violence was used to repress and terrorize enemies of the left, perverts, or racialized minorities; to show the weakness of the state and its inability to maintain order; and to display the total commitment of the fascist militant. Paramilitarism socialized militants into a brotherhood, a comradeship of a "segregated, hardened elite, beyond conventional standards of behavior" (Mann 2004: 29).

Fascist organizations provided a sense of mission and identity. Brazilian Integralism, the largest fascist party in Latin America in the 1930s, "imposed a way of living, behaving, speaking, keeping silent, walking, getting married, dying, and presenting oneself" (Pereira Gonçalves and Caldeira Neto 2022: 29). Members of Brazilian Integralism wore green shirts and greeted each other with the word *Anauê*, meaning "you are my relative." Upon joining they were baptized and swore "unrelenting obedience to the leader ... as well as their commitment to the norms and doctrine of integralism" (20).

Populist organizations allow for the reinforcement of identities of us versus them, communities of the righteous, worldviews, and, in some cases, even a mission to followers tasked with returning power to the people. Yet paramilitarism and physical violence are not organizational features of populism. Populists have created different types of parties that are often personalist, such as informally organized clientelist parties, mass-based parties, television parties, and digital parties. In the Global South populists have organized followers using networks that exchange votes for services. Mass parties have a "mass base which contributes to the functioning of the party both financially and with its political militancy; a large and permanent bureaucracy; a highly hierarchical and centralized organizational structure; a capillary territorial presence ... and an explicit and persistent ideological orientation" (Gerbaudo 2019: 31).

Neoliberal television parties resemble a media or marketing company. Experts in media marketing and communication who appeal to voters as depoliticized consumers replace the full-time bureaucrats of mass-based parties, and the telegenic qualities of a leader take priority over platforms or ideologies. In reaction to these transformations that turned citizens into consumers of television, many demanded increasing direct participation in decisions. Despite using web platforms to increase participation, these parties resorted to plebiscitary democracy so that members could ratify decisions the leadership had already made (Gerbaudo 2019).

The fascist state created a series of institutions and a community of "disciplined, hardened fighters" (Paxton 2005: 143). Populist organizations have been formed from the bottom up, like the Tea Party, or from the top down, as was done by Chávez's government. Regardless of their origins, these organizations promote polarization and politicize social interactions as the confrontation between antagonistic camps.

Performances and Communication Styles

Fascist and populist leaders were media innovators who used radio, cinema, television, and the social web to communicate directly with citizens. As will be explained in detail later, they performed, imagined, and lived politics as extraordinary moments, different from bureaucratized and banal ordinary politics. All spheres of social and personal life could become politicized as arenas for the struggle between two antagonistic camps: the old, dying regime and the new polity, society, and humanity in the making. Extraordinary politics were performed in ceremonies and rituals that celebrated the extraordinariness of the leader, his or her embodiment of the people, while simultaneously creating horizontal bonds of solidarity and identity among the participants. These ceremonies constructed a people against a series of internal and external enemies.

Movements in Power and Regimes

Complex definitions analytically aim to distinguish when these isms' followers are trying to get to power, their actions when they get to office, and whether they can overhaul institutions to create regimes (Arato and Cohen 2022; de la Torre 2019; Paxton 1998). Political institutions often keep fascist and populists at the margins of the political system. Crises of political representation, economic upheavals, or catastrophic events often become opportunities to get to office. Whereas political elites invited Mussolini and Hitler to form coalition governments, thinking that they could control and manage their radicalism, populists got to power by winning elections. Section 5 will elaborate on the different actions that took place under dissimilar institutional contexts that led to the violent and sudden death of democracy under fascist dictatorships, or to the slow undermining of democracy under populism.

Conclusions

Surveying different definitions illustrates the limitations of distinct conceptual strategies. The advantage of minimum definitions is their elegance, and the cost is that complexity is reduced to just one component of these phenomena: ideology, politics, or morality. Complex definitions aim to integrate different aspects that minimum definitions have elaborated, yet the challenge is to produce definitions that are multifaceted and simultaneously useful for comparative analysis. Whereas for some scholars, the goal is to differentiate a cat from a dog in order to increase the clarity that is needed to advance and accumulate knowledge, others argue that theory co-constitutes social reality.

They propose to deal with fuzziness by accepting gradations and to live with definitions that do not necessarily solve for good all ambiguities.

Despite criticisms, these categories will stay in academics, politics, and daily life. Populism connotes a particular political logic of antagonism that transforms rivals into enemies and a leader into the symbol of an array of promises and demands for transformation. Populist legitimacy comes from winning elections, and even though they restrict the rights of their enemies, populists do not physically eliminate them. Fascism replaces democracy with plebiscitary rituals of acclamation and gets rid of fundamental freedoms and rights to privacy, communication, and association.

Perhaps history could provide some answers to gradations and permutations. Finchelstein (2017) has argued that after its military defeat at the end of the war, fascism had run its course and Juan Perón, Getulio Vargas, Jean-Marie, and Marine Le Pen, among others, adapted it to democratic times. Populism became a new type of postwar authoritarianism that accepted elections. Yet, as critics have shown, not all experiences labeled populism have fascist origins. Right and left populism share a political logic based on the existential confrontation between friend and enemy (Laclau 2005). They are in the democratic camp as long as they accept electoral outcomes. When radical right populists do not accept losing elections and organize insurrections and court the support of paramilitary groups, are we experiencing the mutation of right-wing populism into wannabe fascists? Finchelstein (2024) argues that we are living in a new historical time in which leaders like Trump or Bolsonaro do not recognize the legitimacy of elections when they lose, share with fascists appeals to violence and militarization, use lies and conspiracy theories, draw on racism and xenophobia, and attack democracy. Yet because they emerged in a new historical constellation that values democracy, they faced the resistance of organizations of civil society, part of the media, common citizens, political parties that value democracy, and state functionaries, and so have not been allowed to impose fascism.

In the twenty-first century postfascists use but do not depend on paramilitary violence. They have accepted elections, particularly if they win, yet they have not agreed to recognize the legitimacy of political rivals. They use religious and cultural tropes to build enemies of the purity of the people. Differently from political enemies who could be defeated and contained, ethnic-religious enemies might need to be segregated, marginalized, expelled, or even murdered.

The following sections explore the similarities and differences between these isms, and contrast how they eroded or abolished democracy. They distinguish when fascists and populists challenge power, get to office, and can bring regime change. The text uses complex definitions to focus on fascists' and populists' ideologies, organizations, styles of communication, and performances.

3 Similarities

Sections 3 and 4 focus on the similarities and differences between fascism and populism. This contrasts the political logic that constructs democratic subjects accepting pluralism and the confrontation between political rivals whose demands could be solved within existing institutions, with the populist and fascist logic that builds popular subjects. Under the latter a plurality of demands merges, and the social is divided into a confrontation between two antagonistic camps (Laclau 2005). To solve these demands, a rupture of the institutional system might be needed. When contrasted with the political logic of liberal democracy – its legitimation, beliefs, strategies, and practices – fascism and populism give the impression that they are quite similar in how they construct the people as a unitary actor, their notion of leadership as embodiment, and their understanding of politics as extraordinary moments of change, renewal, and liberation. Section 4 will show that, despite these similarities, they are fundamentally different because of their use of violence, legitimation strategies, and historicity.

The People

Fascism and populism are not external viruses that attack democracy from afar; they are part of modernity and the democratization process, and reactions to what are perceived as failures. Fascism and populism offer alternatives to liberal notions of representation. Fascists believe that "genuine democracy was based on identity between the governors and the governed – a principle from which it followed that the popular will could be concentrated in one individual, making a dictatorship such as Mussolini's a much more credible expression of democracy than liberal parliamentarism" (Müller 2011: 116). The Nazis gave facism a racial, more exclusionary, and radical interpretation. "The leader had a mystical connection to his people, but ultimately, he did so because they were of the same 'racial stock' united against an enemy race and its universalist ethical beliefs, which could only weaken the Volks' authentic will" (123). Populists combine the idea that the leader embodies the people and their will with the notion of the centrality of elections as the only legitimate route to get to power. Their reasoning is that because the leader is like the people but inherently superior, the people will only vote for their truthful embodiment, and if electoral results do not confirm their beliefs, it is because elections were rigged.

The concept of the people is ambiguous and yet central to democracy, nationalism, fascism, and populism. "The people" is not an empirical reality located out there waiting to be discovered and analyzed. As Laclau (2005) wrote, "the people" is a social construct that could be imagined differently. This highly emotional term has been used to refer to all the population of a nation or a wannabe nation imagined as a political community in opposition to other nations. Sometimes the nation is attached to the soil, to immemorial times with ancient roots in language, culture, religion, race, or ethnicity that differentiate the truthful members of a national community from "the other" who does not really belong to the homeland. Often the other is imagined as a threat to the rightful members of the people because they could contaminate or soil the purity of their culture, religion, or ethnic and racial makeup. When religion, race, and culture are used to demarcate the in-group from the out-group, there is always the possibility of violence. The politicization of the fear of pollution often leads to the dehumanization of the other or, worse, to genocide. The most extreme examples of the consequences of these constructs were the Nazis' genocide of Jews, gypsies, and other groups racialized as inferior, and Mussolini's brutal colonial wars. Similarly to fascism, but without its genocidal violence, the radical populist right uses religion and culture to construct the other as a polluting threat. In India, Europe, Israel, and the US the Muslim is imagined as the other; in Turkey and Israel the enemies are secular elites; for Trump it is illegal aliens mostly coming from Latin America, and so on.

An alternative construct of "the people" differentiates the rightful citizens who work and produce from parasitical others who appropriate the fruits of the citizens' labor. The opposition then becomes against the few who have monopolized and used economic resources, politics, and culture to marginalize, exploit, or take advantage of the many. Emotions of envy and resentment are used by leftist populists all over the world to depict enemies as oligarchical parasites or as the caste that has appropriated all resources.

Elites loathe and fear the people when imagined as the poor, those at the bottom of society, because the concept of the people evokes strong pictures of the irrational crowd and of the dangerous masses. The notion of the poor denotes a position of "inferiority and subordination, an ascription of lowliness that relegates the poor to a lesser part of society, at the bottom of social life" (Kalyvas 2019: 542). They are constructed as the plebeian, the low, the inferior, the outcast, those lacking education, manners, worth, and merit.

In Argentina in the 1940s, recent immigrants from the interior of the country were despised by upper- and middle-class folks as "greasers" and "little dark heads" (*cabecitas negras*), meaning the "low," nonwhite, and uneducated sectors of the population. The plebeians are those whose voices do not count, who are misplaced and unseen. In "Ten Thesis on Politics" Rancière (2010: 38) wrote, "If there is someone that you do not wish to recognize as a political being, you begin by not seeing him as the bearer of signs of politicity, by not understanding what he says, by not hearing what issues from his mouth as discourse." He had previously argued, "The patricians do not see what is coming from the mouths of the plebeians are articulated words speaking of common things, and not growls of hunger and furor" (Rancière 2000: 12).

Alternatively, the poor and the plebeian could be portrayed as the mythical bearers of virtue. José Álvarez Junco (1987: 251–253) quoted historian of the French Revolution Jules Michelet's exaltation of the people as the "embodiment of two treasures: first is the virtue of sacrifice, and second are instinctual ways of life that are more precious than the sophisticated knowledge of the so-called cultured men." He also reminds us that Mikhail Bakunin wrote, "The people is the only source of moral truth ... and I have in mind the scoundrel, the dregs, uncontaminated by bourgeois civilization."

The notion of the people oscillates between passivity and activity, the female and the male. The people could be portrayed as the submissive object of abuse and women-like because of their passivity. Or the people could be constructed as the virile embodiment of national-popular values and the opposite to effeminate elites. As political theorist Paula Diehl (2023) argues, populism and, I will add, fascism, share in the democratic imagination, offering to transform the passive people into the active bearers of collective national virtues.

Populism and fascism offer a voice to those whose ability to speak does not count, those whose voices appear to the ears of elites as mere noise. Both are transgressive of the proper way of doing politics, and of whom has the education, manners, and speech capacities to participate in the public sphere. Roger Eatwell (2007: 8) writes, "Hitler used a form of low rather than high language, the discourse of ordinary people rather than the grandiloquence of the political Establishment." Borrowing from Pierre Ostiguy (2017: 76), populists and fascists perform "the celebratory desecration of the 'high.' They 'flaunt the low' to show the illegitimacy of the domination of elites, and the artificiality of their symbols of distinction in their 'manners, demeanors, way of speaking and dressing, vocabulary, and tastes displayed in public'" (78).

Fascists and populists conceive the people hierarchically as made up of leaders and followers. "The people" has one voice and will that ultimately is that of the leader. Under fascism and populism, a leader claims to be the embodiment of the popular, the plebeian, and national values. Fascist and populist leaders offer their protection and to be the voice of the marginalized, the oppressed, and the uncounted in exchange for their loyalty and devotion. Differently from populism or fascism, democratic plebeian politics and cultures of resistance are bottom up, leaderless, and based on the disunity of the voices of the many (Breaugh 2019; Kalyvas 2019). Drawing on Rancière, Benjamín Arditi (2015: 102–104) suggests analyzing the people as an event, an unexpected eruption of collective action by means of which those who are not seen and do not have a recognized and legitimate voice demand to be heard as equals in the public sphere. The people as an event refers to those occasional moments when those at the bottom and whose voices do not count say they have had enough and refuse to accept their place "when that place wrongs their equality" (106). Such an event differs from populist and fascist politics because it is plural, leaderless, and bottom up.

Democrats, fascists, and populists construct differently the notion of the people's will. Political theorist Paulina Ochoa (2015: 74–75) writes that democrats use notions of self-limitation and in the name of the people place limits on their claims to be their spokespersons. They conceive of the people as indeterminate, accept "that the people can (and probably will) change," that their "appeal to the people's will is fallible, temporary, and incomplete." Democrats acknowledge that their "claims may be wrong and accept political defeats." On the contrary, the fascist leader is the bearer of the infallible truth. Fascists abolish elections, replacing them with plebiscitary ceremonies of acclamation. Populists do not abolish democracy because their legitimacy lies in winning elections. Yet they contend that because they are the only truthful voice of the people, they do not need to limit their claims. They "assume that the will of the mythical 'people' is transparent, fixed in time, and available for a leader to incarnate its will" (de la Torre 2015: 20).

Fascists and populists (right and left) build the people-as-one as "an absolute collective individual with a single will, transparent to itself" (Kalyvas 2019: 547). The assertion that populism constructs the people-as-one is contested by scholars who differentiate right and left populism in terms of whether they construct a unitary or plural people. Paola Biglieri and Luciana Cadahia (2021: 35) differentiate right-wing populism, which they call postfascism because they imagine the people as one, from populism in the singular, which is left-wing populism because the people "is not a unit understood as a self-enclosed identity that expels differences." These scholars conveniently forget that, under leftist populism, at times of confrontation the leader appropriates the claim to be the only voice of the people. After winning a referendum against drastic cuts in social services and government expending, Alexis Tsipras, the leader of Syriza, capitulated to the demands of the Troika and imposed severe budget cuts in 2015. Under Evo Morales, the constitution was changed to recognize Bolivia as a pluri-national state composed of different Indigenous original peoples, as well as whites, Afro-descendants, and mixed-blood citizens. When Indigenous people challenged Morales's policies of natural resource extraction, they were labeled as not truly Indigenous and manipulated by foreign NGOs (Postero 2015). In sum, fascist and populist leaders and their coterie name who belongs to the nation and the people, and spell out the traits of the popular.

Notions of peoplehood inform nation-building projects and policies. The allure of fascism is its "message of national renewal, powerfully linking fear and hope" (Kershaw 2015: 230). The unity, even the identity, of the nation is gained "from the 'cleansing' of all those deemed not to belong" (229). Fascists use militarism and terror to get rid of internal enemies who corrupt the nation such as communists, Jews, and other undesirables, and war to conquer living space, as did the Aryan Germans so they could colonize Eastern Europe and as did the Italians so they could take Libya and Ethiopia.

Latin American populists in the 1940s and 1950s imagined the nation as mestizo, meaning cultural and racial hybrids of white, Indigenous, and black. They saw that their role was to slowly assimilate Indigenous people, Afrodescendants, and mixed-race poor people to a nation that over time would become increasingly culturally and racially white. The notion of *mestizaje* was thus an exclusionary project of inclusion as nonwhite cultures needed to be abandoned to become a member of the mestizo nation. Mestizaje, particularly in Brazil, led to the myth that Latin American nations were democracies free of racism.

Women's role under fascism and populism was to reproduce and morally educate healthy members of the nation. Their policies supported maternity and child benefits for large families. Fascists and populists created organizations to teach women their responsibilities in reproduction, education, and consumption. They opened job opportunities in female service and teaching professions, while creating party branches for women. The Nazis' women's section had more than 2 million members in 1938 (Passmore 2014: 128). The women's section of the Peronist party boasted 500,000 members, and women massively voted for Perón and his ticket in 1951 after Perón gave them the right to vote (Plotkin 2003: 179).

Leadership

The question of leadership has been at the center of fascist and populist scholarship. Whereas some scholars have focused on the social conditions that produce charisma (Germani 1978; Parsons 1942), others have focused on the charismatic bond (de la Torre 2022; Eatwell 2007; Pappas 2021; Pinto and Larsen 2007; Zuquete 2007, 2008). Parsons (1942: 138) wrote that rapid social change led to "widespread psychological insecurity and anxiety. Charismatic movements of various sorts seem to function in the situation as mechanisms of reintegration which give large number of common people imbued with a high emotional, indeed often fanatical zeal for a cause." Parsons and Germani differentiated rational action from anomic and irrational action provoked by rapid social change or catastrophes that broke down social integration. Hence organization and rational action are the opposites of disorganization under which charismatic leaders appeal to and mobilize disorganized and irrational masses in a state of anomie. Approaches that reduce emotions to irrational responses were criticized by scholars who focus on organizations and political opportunities.

When studying charisma, the challenge is not to reduce followers to irrational masses or charisma to the attribute of an individual. In what follows, I rely on reconceptualization of the charismatic bond (Eatwell 2007; Pinto and Larsen 2007; Zuquete 2007, 2008) and on my reconstruction of Weber's notion of charisma as a social relationship (de la Torre 2023). Eatwell distinguishes contagion charisma based on an intensively emotional bond with a leader, from coterie charisma, "the attraction to a hard core of supporters, both in their inner courts and more locally, who have held that the leader was driven by a special mission and/or that the leader was invested with unique powers" (Eatwell 2007: 15). I focus on the redemptive mission of the leader and on the body of the leader in order to study charisma as a social relation. Differently from Parsons and Germani, these approaches do not counterpose charisma to organization. On the contrary, they argue that to be successful, charismatic appeals need to coincide with organizations.

The Redemptive Mission of the Leader

Differently from rational bureaucratic leaders whose legitimacy lies in their office, "the bearer of charisma enjoys loyalty and authority by virtue of a mission believed to be embodied in him" (Weber 1978: 1117). Followers project onto leaders their own beliefs, wishes, and desires. Pinto and Larsen (2007: 133), in their conclusion to their book on fascism and charisma, wrote:

> [E]very fascist dictator had to possess some individual abilities that made them "extraordinary." He needed followers to "understand" or "appreciate" and connect these qualities. Finally, there must be a situation or an event that which required these unusual abilities, or which could "call" for the reconstruction of the regime in such a way as to allow the application of new solutions to problems.

The missions of leaders are "often linked to a foundation myth, in which leaders like Mussolini portray themselves as the creators of radical new movements" (Eatwell 2007: 6). Similarly, Perón claimed to have developed *justicialismo* and Chávez's socialism of the twenty-first century as alternatives to communism and liberal capitalism. The leader must prove charismatic "in the eyes of their adherents" (Weber 1978: 1112). Hitler led Germany "from the depths of a depression to full employment" (Mosse 1999: 38). Mussolini and Hitler reached the peak of their popularity in 1935 6 when Italy conquered

Abyssinia and in 1939–41 when Germany occupied most of Europe (Eatwell 2007: 10). When Hugo Chávez in a televised broadcast accepted his responsibility for leading an unsuccessful coup attempt in 1992 against President Carlos Andrés Pérez, he became the symbol of the struggle against the corrupt neoliberal political establishment. Venezuelans subsequently voted massively for Chávez in December 1998.

Charismatic leaders invoke and are linked to myths. Some myths are religiously inspired; others are more secular. Hitler used Christian symbols such as "the resurrection of the German Reich," the "blood of martyrs," and constant appeals to Providence (Mosse 1999: 74). His mission was to restore Germany's greatness. He manufactured an aura of divine infallibility. Hitler, for example claimed, "I hereby set forth for myself and my successors in the leadership of the Party the claim of political infallibility. I hope the world will grow as accustomed to that claim as it has to the claim of the Holy Father" (Finchelstein 2024: 76). Donald Trump triumphed in two mythical and almost religious arenas of American capitalism: the business world and mass entertainment. His name was a brand for casinos, steaks, hotels, and other commodities. He was a media celebrity hosting the TV series *The Apprentice* for fourteen seasons, and before winning the presidency he was a regular host on *Fox & Friends*.

The Body of the Leader

Weber (1978: 1112) wrote that charismatic leaders are "bearers of specific gifts of the body and mind that were considered 'supernatural' (in the sense that not everybody could have access to them)." Contemporaries referred to "the piercing power of Mussolini's eyes" and were "mesmerized by Hitler's power of oratory" (Eatwell 2007: 9).

After reaching power the body of the fascist or populist leader becomes omnipresent. More than a thousand films and newsreels were made that feature the Führer (Eatwell 2007: 13). Similarly, in Argentina, Juan and Eva Perón were constantly in the newsreels, their images were on billboards and posters, and their voices were on the radio. Chávez had a weekly six-hour TV and radio program in which he sang, cracked jokes, attacked internal and external enemies, and informed citizens about crucial policies. Donald Trump's image was everywhere as well. He dominated the news cycle and was constantly on social media.

Some leaders bragged about the hypermasculinities manifested in their success in sports, in the business world, in the military, or as "conquerors" of women. Some were portrayed as fathers of their nations. Getulio Vargas claimed to be "the father of the poor," while Lázaro Cárdenas was "tata Lázaro." The father metaphor "turns citizens into permanent children. It turns a politician into someone who understands the interests of citizens – even when they do not – and who may punish wayward children who fail to recognize their wisdom" (Kampwirth 2010: 12).

Extraordinary Politics, Mass Meetings, and the Charisma of Rhetoric

Fascists and populists offer redemption from the routines of day-to-day administrative politics that lay in the hands of bureaucrats and experts. Under fascism and populism politics is performed, imagined, and lived as extraordinary moments of redemption against bureaucratized and banalized ordinary politics. Mass meetings are the arenas in which the leader is recognized and acclaimed by followers. These are the sites for "the recognition on the part of those subject to authority which is decisive for the validity of charisma" (Weber 1978: 242). With the repetition of songs, slogans, and banners, mass meetings aim to create political identities or to at least differentiate the in-group from the out-group. In these meetings the people validate the authority of the leader and create horizontal links of belonging to a camp against a series of enemies.

Mass meetings were a key fascist innovation that influenced Latin American populists. When Juan Perón, José María Velasco Ibarra, and Jorge Eliécer Gaitán lived in or visited Italy and Germany, they attended, were inspired by, and emulated Mussolini's and Hitler's mass meetings. Populist leaders understood politics as the people's participation in mass meetings, their occupation of public spaces, and demonstrations on behalf of a leader. Mass gatherings became crucial mechanisms to create horizontal links. The French National Front and later the Rassemblement National, for example, organized rituals to build a community of militant believers. These included a yearly tribute to Joan of Arc, the celebration of the colors of France, summer schools, mass rallies, and feasts. These rituals reinforce feelings of belonging. For its activists the Front is a community of patriots under siege by the enemies of the fatherland. They play key roles in mobilizing the vote and spreading the party's ideology. Their duty is not only to convince but to convert. Jean-Marie Le Pen asserted that the militant "has to recruit others who in turn recruit others in order to make a snowball that will end up being the majority" (Zúquete 2007: 104).

Contrary to predictions that mass meetings will disappear with television and social media, Donald Trump's 2016, 2020, and 2024 campaigns made ample use of mass rallies. He claimed to be "the only man without a guitar that can fill a stadium" (Wolff 2021: 201). His rallies resembled sport events where people had fun at tailgate parties. Trump danced, cracked jokes, insulted rivals, and used violent words and incitation to attack opponents.

Weber (1978: 1130) wrote that stump speeches prioritize rhetoric over content and are "purely emotional." Rhetoric "has the same meaning as the street parades and festivals: to imbue the masses with the notion of the party's power and confidence in victory and, above all, to convince them of the leader's charismatic qualifications." Weber also differentiated between scientific and political speeches. "The enterprise of the prophet is closer to that of the popular leader (demagogos) or the political publicist than that of the teacher" (445). Building on Weber, José Álvarez Junco (1987: 220) wrote political discourse "does not inform or explain, but persuades and shapes attitudes ... It responds to areas of disquiet and problems, it offers reassurance." Since the goal is to motivate people to act, "well-reasoned arguments are less useful than emotional appeals" (Álvarez Junco 1990: 234).

To be successful in performing politics as extraordinary moments of change and renewal, charisma needs to go together with organizations. Mussolini and Hitler came to power with the support of an extensive network of uncivil society made of war veteran organizations, extreme nationalists, and other undemocratic groups (Eatwell 2007). When leaders do not form organizations, their movements vanish after their death. José María Velasco Ibarra was president of Ecuador five times, dominating politics from the 1930s to the early 1970s. He finished only one term in office because he was overthrown by military coups, yet he returned four times to office as the "Great Absentee." Instead of creating a political party, he gathered the support of politicians and their clientelist networks and did not create organizations seeking the endorsement of existing associations of civil society. Hence, after he died, Velasquismo evaporated (de la Torre 2010). Differently, Perón co-opted or repressed labor leaders to create his own coterie. He organized a political party and put together a women's branch. His movement did not die with him, and when allowed by the military left, right-wing Peronists have dominated Argentinean politics.

Nationalism, fascism, and populism advocated for a "democracy of the masses in which the people would in theory directly govern themselves" (Mosse 1999: 2). Fascism inaugurated "a new a new kind of politics designed to mobilize the masses and to integrate them into a political system – through rites and ceremonies in which they could participate, and through an aesthetic of politics which appealed to the longing for community and comradeship in an industrial age" (92). Populists combined a rhetoric that portrayed the people as antagonist to elites or the oligarchy with collective action to intimidate opponents and to show the power of the people. Populist followers occupied public spaces from which they were often marginalized; they did not consider that political rivals have the right to express themselves, and they silenced such rivals. The legacy of the populist incorporation of those previously excluded as the people, while empowering the many, went against the rights of expression not only of the few, but of any critic of the leader who could be transformed into an enemy. As in fascism their participation in mass meetings gave them the sense of their transformation from spectators into protagonists of their own history. Yet, similarly to fascism the script was written by the leader and at most by some of his close collaborators.

Fascism and some populisms create political religions understood as offering redemption through politics. They offer "a comprehensive set of meanings, but also spectacles and rituals, which competed with those of the Catholic Church in particular" (Müller 2011: 113). As Arato (2015) wrote, the power left vacant by theological or religious categories like God or Christ is replaced by human agents such as class in Marxism, and the people and the leader in fascism and populism. These human agents are not only endowed with the category of sacredness but are credited with supernatural traits. "Hitler frequently talked about himself as an instrument of 'Providence,' and some of his orations about 'faith in my Volk' actually concluded with the word 'Amen'" (Müller 2011: 113). Hitler was a leader for life. He was "the leader of the party, the army, and the people. In his person the power of the state, the people, and the movement were unified" (Neumann 1944: 84). Joseph Goebbels said that Hitler is "the naturally creative instrument of divine destiny" (Finchelstein 2024: 58). One of the thousands of letters sent to Mussolini every day portrayed him as godlike. "For us Italians you are our God on earth, and we turn to you faithful and certain of being heard" (Kershaw 2015: 281).

Juan and Eva Perón were similarly transformed into religious figures. Evita asserted that "Perón is a God," while Peronists professed that "God is Peronist" (Finchelstein 2014: 80). Hugo Chávez became the synthesis of Jesus and Simón Bolívar, the liberator of Latin America. González Trejo (2018: 139–141) writes that after his death, Chávez was buried in a newly built secular sanctuary that "symbolizes the renaissance of the homeland and the immeasurable life of the Eternal Commandant." Chávez's coffin has the inscription "Supreme Commander of the Bolivarian Revolution." Above his sarcophagus in the center is a portrait of Bolívar the Father with one of Chávez his Son on its right and left sides.

When Jair Bolsonaro was stabbed during the presidential campaign in 2018, his Pentecostal, Christian, and Catholic followers prayed for his prompt recovery, and "religious leaders said that God had protected Brazil's savior" (de la Torre and Srisa-nga 2022: 32). Christian fundamentalist followers constructed Trump as God's emissary, a quasi-providential conductor destined to save America. His White House press secretary Sarah Sanders said, "I think God calls all of us to fill different roles at different times, and I think he wanted Donald Trump to be president" (Finchelstein 2020: 92). One of Trump's

Christian supporters maintained, "Millions of Americans believe the election of President Donald Trump represented God giving us another chance – perhaps our last chance to truly make America great again" (94). Trump argued in 2016 that because his leadership comes from the divine, this is "a struggle for the survival of our nation, believe me. And this will be our last chance to save it." His election, he said, represented "our Independence Day" (97). His 2024 campaign released a video entitled *God Made Trump*.

> God had to have someone willing to go into the den of vipers. Call out the fake news for their tongues as sharp as a serpent's. The poison of vipers is on their lips. So God made Trump. God said, "I will need someone who will be strong and courageous. Who will not be afraid or terrified of wolves when they attack. A man who cares for the flock. A shepherd to mankind who won't ever leave or forsake them. I need the most diligent worker to follow the path and remain strong in faith. And know the belief in God and country.[3]

If leaders are portrayed as godlike, enemies become dehumanized and the embodiment of pollution, of all that is wrong, even evil. The Nazis made their fantasies about their enemies come true.

> If anti-Semitic lies stated that Jews were inherently dirty and contagious and therefore ought to be killed, the Nazis created conditions in the ghettos and concentration camps where dirtiness and widespread disease became reality. Starved, tortured, and radically dehumanized, Jewish inmates became what the Nazis had planned for them to become and were, accordingly, killed. (Finchelstein 2024: 59)

Conclusions

This section focused on some of the parallels between these isms. Other similarities could be added and explained such as their claim to offer a third way of development that overcame the failures of both communism and capitalist-liberal democracy, or their assertions to be beyond right–left binaries. As in the 1920s and 1930s when conservative elites normalized and sanitized fascists, inviting them to form coalition governments under the false assumption that they would tame their radicalism, conservative elites are forming coalitions with the extreme right in the twenty-first century. In the 1920s and 1930s Italian and German elites invited fascists to the executive office. Republican elites allowed Trump to become a candidate and refused to get rid of him even after his supporters used violence to storm Congress. The Argentinean right-wing party Together for Change joined Milei in the runoff

---

[3] www.nytimes.com/2024/01/17/opinion/trump-god-evangelicals-anointed.html.

election against the Peronist ticket, and its former presidential candidate Patricia Bullrich and other figures of the "respectable right" are in key ministries.

Historian Robert Paxton (1998: 10) writes that comparison "works better when we try to account for differences than when we try to amass vague resemblances." The similarities between fascism and populism analyzed in this section make sense when contrasted with how liberal democrats understand key categories of political life like the people, leadership, or their notion of the political. Democrats understand politics as based on pluralism and the nonantagonistic confrontation between political rivals who ought to be convinced by the logic of the best argument. Differently, fascists and populists face and/or built existential enemies. The notion of the enemy that ought to be contained leads to a political logic that gives priority to confrontation and polarization and that aims to get rid of the other. The next two sections will show that despite sharing a non-pluralistic view of politics, performances of politics as extraordinary moments of renewal, views of the people as one, and leadership as the charismatic mission to bring redemption, these isms are profoundly different.

4 Differences

Despite the aforementioned resemblances, fascism and populism are distinct political phenomena. The rise of Juan Perón in Argentina helps illuminate their differences. As mentioned in the introduction, when Perón first got to power in 1943 he was a member of a pro-Axis junta that wanted to Christianize the country, making Catholic education mandatory, repressing the left, and banning political parties. The junta was supported by a web of Argentinean clerical-fascist and nationalist groups. As the secretary of labor, he used repression and co-optation to replace independent labor leaders with a cadre of sympathetic bosses, sponsored unionization, and met some union demands. Perón ditched fascism when he realized that after the defeat of the Axis, elections were the only mechanism to legitimately get to power. Even though he admired Mussolini, he said fascism was "an unrepeatable phenomenon, a classic style to define a precise and determined epoch" (Finchelstein 2017: 12). In 1946 Perón won the presidency in an open and clean election. Differently from fascists, Perón kept violence for the most part at the rhetorical level. I write for the most part because his supporters tried to burn newspaper buildings and churches and beat up rivals in the streets, and his regime incarcerated opponents. Yet compared to fascism, state violence was lighter. When Perón was overthrown by the military, these juntas were much more repressive than his administration. Differently from fascists, populist did not use generalized violence to eliminate enemies and relied on elections as the only legitimate tool to get to office, meaning that rights to information and association were constrained but not abolished.

This section focuses on their different uses of violence and their strategies of legitimation, and argues that whereas fascism emerged in a particular historical constellation and that what came after was postfascism, populism cannot be confined to a particular historical moment.

Violence and the Construction of Friend and Enemy

Even tough populists and fascists imagined the people as one, and right-wing populists like fascists used ethnic-cultural and religious constructs; these movements differed in their use of violence to deal with external and internal enemies. Fascists "idealized war as the laboratory of a form of civilization organized by the total state and embodied in the new humanity that emerged from the trenches" (Traverso 2016: 99). Their objective was to rebuild the nation by violently getting rid of enemies, and by taking revenge against those responsible for the humiliation of the motherland. The carriers of the cleansing of enemies and the regeneration of nation were the new fascist men. They ought to be "energetic, courageous, and spartan ... the very opposite of muddleheaded, talkative, intellectualizing liberals and socialists – the exhausted, tired old men of the old order" (Mosse 1999: 31). Fascist virility was opposed to "all symptoms of decadence: weakness, cowardice, immorality, ugliness, monstrosity" that characterized the Jewish and homosexual outsiders (Traverso 2016: 210).

Fascists' supporters and leaders were young. Many were former frontline soldiers who had become "immune to the horrors of war" (Mosse 1999: 15) and wanted to use warlike methods against internal enemies "that must be defeated and destroyed" (Gentile 2008: 292). When violence was successful in silencing and terrorizing enemies and was unpunished, it "had both cathartic and a liberating effect on the perpetrator ... reinforcing their collective sense of being a segregated, hardened elite, beyond conventional standards of behavior" (Mann 2004: 29).

Fascist violence had its origin in the biologically racist dehumanization of the nonwhite native as an inherently inferior and primitive other during colonialism and imperialism (Traverso 2003). European intellectuals provided rationalizations for colonial and racist projects, and for the genocide of nonwhite populations. Historian Enzo Traverso reports that during the second half of the nineteenth century approximately 50–60 million died as victims of imperialist and colonialist violence and genocide. For example, the population of the Belgian Congo was cut by half from 20 million to 10 million between 1880 and 1920 (65).

Michael Mann (2004: 16) distinguishes political cleansing whose violence ends when the enemies surrender from ethnic cleansing that leads to the genocide of ethnically defined enemies constructed as agents of pollution and hence as inassimilable. If the people understood as an ethnos is to rule itself, then what to do with those casted as essentially different and even as polluting because of their ethnicity, religion, and culture? The search for "ethnic unity might outweigh the kind of citizen diversity that is central to democracy" (3).

Franz Nuemann (1944: 103) writes that long before Hitler, a "biological race theory replaced the political theory of nationality." Racism and anti-Semitism substituted for class struggle. "By heaping all hatred, all resentment, all misery upon an enemy who can easily be exterminated and who cannot resist, Aryan society can be integrated as a whole" (125). Nazism was a unique and more brutal form of fascism because of its extreme biologization of anti-Semitism and its insistence on the need to eliminate the Jew to regenerate the nation (Traverso 2003). For the Nazis, the image of the Jew incorporated constructs of a racially distinct other and a carrier of the disease of "Communist subversion." Hitler referred to the "Jewish bacillus" as a hotbed of revolutionary infection, arguing that repression alone was inadequate unless it also included a racial purge (Traverso 2003: 120). Anti-Semitism became a violent crusade to eliminate the Jew to purify the nation and to free it from Communism. Nazism, as Traverso (150) writes, was a synthesis of science, irrational myth, and various forms of violence. The Jewish genocide was "conceived and realized as part of a total war, a war of conquest that was both 'racial' and colonial, and extremely radical" (75).

Fascist violence emerged in a political and cultural milieu in which both left and right praised revolutionary physical force to get rid of parliamentarism in order to create a better society. It also took place at political conjunctures when the state could not or was unwilling to impose its monopoly over the use of violence. Fascist paramilitary groups were tolerated by the state and used by elites to confront and defeat the threat of Bolshevism. Praise for violence was also expressed in political theory. Carl Schmitt's notion of the political did not identify violence with a pre-political state of nature but transformed it into the very core of the political that was defined as the existential conflict between friend and enemy, always implying the possibility of death. "The essential task of politics for Schmitt is not to hide but to develop conflict" (Traverso 2016: 199). As Franz Neumann (1944: 45) wrote, "This is a doctrine of brute force in its most striking form, one that sets itself against every aspect and act of liberal democracy and against our whole traditional conception of the governance of law."

Populist violence was different. Perón described himself as a "herbivorous lion," meaning that his violent tropes against enemies remained, for the most part, at the rhetorical level (Finchelstein 2020: 100). Yet symbolic and verbal violence was used to ridicule, marginalize, and force critics into silence or exile. Populists also used physical violence beating up opponents, and even tried to destroy the symbols that marked their exclusion from the public sphere that were in the hands of elites like universities and newspaper buildings in Perón's Argentina. From Perón to Chávez, Latin American populists could beat up, incarcerate, or exile enemies, but they did not rely on violence to clean their nations of enemies.

American populists like George Wallace and Donald Trump performed mass meetings in which violence could be a possible outcome. In Wallace's unsuccessful bids for the presidency in 1964, 1968, and 1972, "violent antagonism played a particular strong role ... the threat, and anticipation, and performance of which was central to his image and success" (Lowndes 2005: 148). In a 2016 campaign rally, pointing to a critic, Trump said, "There is a remnant left over there. Maybe get the remnant out. Get the remnant out. The crowd, taking its cue, then tried to root out other people who might be dissenters, all the while crying 'USA'" (Snyder 2017: 45). In another he said, "'I'd like to punch him in the face.' 'Knock the crap out of him, would you? I promise you I will pay the legal fees'" (Hochschild 2016: 224).

Differently from the populist performance of the possibility of violence used to create feelings of comradeship among supporters under the tutelage of a leader, Trump and Bolsonaro took violence to a new level when they refused to accept that they lost elections and their followers took over the symbols of state power. Did these actions show that the boundaries between fascism – or, if you prefer, postfascism – and right-wing populism are becoming murkier and there is a sort of a return to fascists' use of violence? After all, Trump and Bolsonaro, like interwar fascists, were supported by armed militias, but unlike them, have not created militia parties.

Focusing on how enemies are constructed allows us to explore continuities between fascist and populist violence. Finchelstein (2014: 41) shows how the fascist-clerical notion of the total enemy "that must be expelled from the political realm" was reworked by three authoritarian governments in Argentina: the Uriburu dictatorship (1930–2), Peronism (1946–55), and the military dictatorship (1976–83). The military junta built on the notion of the subversive as a total enemy to systematically kidnap, torture, and kill about thirty thousand Argentineans. Subversives were "seen as a virus that needed to be eliminated" (Finchelstein 2014: 126). Thus they were put in concentration camps and tortured, and their offspring taken away and given for adoption by military families.

The construct of "gender ideology" fabricated and popularized by the Catholic Church, similarly to the notion of the subversive, allows for the creation of an identifiable and perverse total enemy that is attempting to destroy the nuclear, heterosexual, and patriarchal family conceived as the basic and most fundamental unit of society. Pope Francis in 2014 talked about the crisis of the family that, according to him, is "an anthropological fact, and consequently a social, cultural fact ... Family is family" (Butler 2024: 76). Gender ideology puts in the same basket different demands for rights such as abortion, access to reproductive technology, sex education, same-sex marriage, gender-conforming surgery, trans rights, etcetera. It provokes the fear that "normal people" understood as gender conforming and hetero will be stripped away from their status as "mother, father, man, or woman, that such words will no longer be speakable," or will be used "for nefarious purposes" (255). When struggles against rights are framed with words such as *gender ideology*, passions are intensified, "stoking fear and redirecting it as hatred, moralizing sadism, and figuring their ... destruction as promise of redemption" (132). To protect the family, those who are advocating for its destruction should be identified, stripped of rights, and even expelled as carriers of a virus. Similarly, the image of the Muslim immigrant in Europe and the illegal alien in the US evokes feelings of invasion, contamination of culture, and pollution of mores. The other constructed as the carrier of strange cultures and religious beliefs, or as perverts that aim to debauch the family become targets of repulsion, fear, and hatred that ought to be chastened and even sacrificed to rebuild the nation.

Populist and Fascist Legitimacy

Fascist believed that "elections distorted true representation" (Finchelstein 2020: 82) because electoral representation could not express popular sovereignty. In his critique of parliamentarism, Schmitt argued that "parliamentary discussion is today nothing more than a device for registering decisions previously reached on the outside" (Neumann 1944: 43), and proposed to replace it with decisionism, "the demand for action instead of deliberation, for decision instead of evaluation" (45). Differently from the plural citizens of a parliamentary democracy, who "voted to choose a fellow citizen to serve as their representatives, fascists expressed their citizenship directly by participating in ceremonies of mass assent" (Paxton 2005: 78–79). "The general will of the people, if not mediated through representative government, needed coherence, and political as well as personal conformity were essential to the existence of such direct democracy" (Mosse 1999: 79). As will be described in the next section, after conservative elites invited Mussolini and Hitler to be part of coalition governments, they outmaneuvered mainstream conservatives, got rid of elections, abolished civil liberties and the free media, and used the state to try to swallow civil society.

For populists, the only legitimate source of power comes from clean elections, and even though they make it difficult for rivals to win, they respect outcomes. Populism incorporates the democratic principle that the only form of legitimacy lies in the vote, with the view of democracy as participation in ceremonies, demonstrations, and other mass rituals that create community, belonging, and identity. These two understandings of democracy are in tension. Whereas for free elections, civil liberties, pluralism, a free press, and rights of association are a necessary precondition, populist mass meetings and ceremonies create a sense of community and even identity among populists by targeting enemies. Populists often do not respect the right of the other to have different opinions and used physical violence to silence them. Yet, differently from fascism, which physically eliminated enemies, populists keep their struggles for the most part at the level of symbolic and discursive violence.

Populists reduce democratic accountability to the notion of clean elections. After winning elections populist leaders feel free to do as they please. In the 1940s Perón said, "We have given the people the opportunity to choose, in the cleanest election in the history of Argentina, between us and our opponents. The people have elected us, so the problem is resolved. What we want is now done in the Republic of Argentina" (Peruzzotti 2013: 75). Populists conceive of state institutions of horizontal accountability such as the comptroller, prosecutors, or anti-corruption agencies as mechanisms of elite control that attempt to dilute the will of the people (Peruzzotti 2023). They argue that in the name of controlling the executive, elites undermine projects of democratization that infringe on the privileges of the few. Populists have replaced mechanisms of horizontal accountability with other branches of government with "variants of 'vertical accountability' involving frequent elections, referenda, and plebiscites" (de la Torre and Arnson 2013: 10).

Democrats, fascists, and populists have different understandings of legitimate power. In what follows I quote our most recent elaboration on their distinct notions of legitimacy borrowing on and developing Claude Lefort's theory.

> In monarchies the king, like God, had two bodies and the two were inseparable. The king's body was mortal, as well as immortal and eternal. Once the body of the king and the body of the politic were decapitated during the democratic revolutions of the 18th century, the space occupied by the religious political body of the king was opened. "Power appears as an empty place and those who exercise it as merely mortals who occupy it only temporarily or who could install themselves in it only by force or cunning." (Lefort 1986: 303)
>
> > The uncertainty of democracy, where power belongs to the people in the abstract but not to a concrete individual who at most could occupy it only

temporarily, could lead to its destruction. The revolutions of the eighteenth century, according to Lefort, also generated "from the outset the principle that would threaten the emptiness of that space: popular sovereignty in the sense of a subject incarnated in a group, however extensive, a stratum however poor, and an institution or a person, however popular." (Arato 2012: 23)

Totalitarianism, thus, "is an attempt to reincarnate society in the figure of a leader or a party which would annul the social division and would realize the fantasy of people-as-one, in which there is no legitimate opposition, where all factual opposition is conceived of as coming from the outside, the enemy" (Flynn 2013: 31). Symbolically, this is done by abandoning the democratic imagination of the people as "heterogeneous, multiple, and in conflict" and by living in a society where power does not belong to any individual (Lefort 1986: 297). Under totalitarianism, there are no internal divisions within the people. The divide is between the people – imagined as having one identity and one will – and its external enemies, which need to be eliminated to maintain the healthy body of the people.

> Populism aims to get rid of the uncertainties of democratic politics by naming a leader as the embodiment of the people and nation. Yet this attempt is different from fascism which abolished democracy altogether. The vote for populists is the only tool to legitimately get to power, therefore democratic uncertainty is not fully abolished. The populist imaginary thus lies between democracy and fascist and Communist totalitarianism. The political theorist Isidoro Cheresky (2015) argued that power in populism is semi-embodied because populists claim legitimacy through winning elections that they could conceivably lose and thus are bound to electoral results. (de la Torre and Srisa-nga 2022: 107–108)

Because populists imagined the people as having one unified voice and will, it is "morally impossible" that they could vote for those constructed as the enemies of the people (Ochoa 2015: 83). When populists lose, or even if they imagine that they won't win elections, they cry electoral fraud or claim elections were rigged. José María Velasco Ibarra, after losing an election in 1940, organized a failed military insurrection that ended with his exile from Ecuador; yet, after four years, an insurrection of the left and the right against the liberal party brought him back to power as the "Great Absentee" (de la Torre 2010). Manuel López Obrador cried fraud the two times he lost elections because, he argued, how could the people vote for another candidate? His followers in protest took over the main streets of Mexico City for weeks (Ochoa 2015). The question is, then, why do some populists abide by the rules of the democratic game knowing that they can lose or win elections, accept defeat, and transfer power peacefully, while others only accept elections if they win? Perhaps, like other politicians they abide by the democratic rules of the game when the stakes of elections are not high. But populists paint elections as crucial moments when the destiny of the nation is at stake, and the choice is between the rebirth of the people and the motherland or its downfall and disintegration.

The Historicity of Fascism and Populism

Sociologist Mabel Berezin (2019: 356) wrote that these isms differ in that "fascism is best conceived as a historical event, whereas populism is an analytical category." Despite profound disagreements, scholars of fascism agree that it was a particular moment in history – the interwar period of the twentieth century – and that whatever came later was postfascism. Fascism was the product of a unique conjuncture. First, fascism emerged after the horrors of the First World War banalized death. Fascists exalted war as "the supreme moment of life, exalting battle as a kind of fulfillment for man and for the triumph of strength, speed, and courage" (Traverso 2003: 94). Second, as argued earlier in this Element, the origins of fascist violence lay in the colonial and imperialist invention of races to dehumanize, exploit, and even kill the nonwhite other. Third, the Bolshevik Revolution was for many a major threat to the social order, and fascists presented themselves as the only force capable of stopping communism. Fourth, fascism emerged during a crisis of political representation and popular consent of constitutional democracy. Right-wing and left-wing intellectuals, activists, and citizens alike praised violence and dictatorship. Corporatism was developed as an alternative form of representation to individualistic liberalism, and as a "forced integration of organized interest, mainly independent unions" (Pinto 2020: 7). The Catholic Church and its intellectuals and organization diffused corporatism as a Christian answer to correct the excesses of liberal capitalism, and as an alternative to atheistic communism. Fascist notions of personalization of leadership, a single party, and organic-statist legislatures were selectively adapted and adopted globally. Salazar in Portugal and Getulio Vargas in Brazil used fascist parties to consolidate their power, to later repress them, and to selectively adopt parts of the fascist playbook like corporatism (Pinto 2020). Fascists got to power in states with weakened old regimes and "half institutionalized democratic parliaments" (Mann 2004: 365). Facism "emerged as a new and audacious synthesis, one that combined radical authoritarianism, militarized activism, and the drive for a coercive state, professing a radical nationalist, imperialist, and racial creed, shaped by violent antipathy against liberals, democrats and socialists" (Elley 2013: 208).

Differently from earlier historicist theories of populism that argued that populism took place during the transition to modernity or in the phase of import substitution industrialization in Latin America, nowadays most scholars do not restrict populism to a historical period. Populist movements and parties have emerged in different socioeconomic, geographical, historical, and institutional settings when citizens have felt that elites have appropriated popular sovereignty. Populists have been elected to govern under different institutional conditions, and in regimes with different levels of legitimacy. As will be explained in Section 5, only when all institutions such as political parties, the courts of justice, parliament, the media, etcetera, lost legitimacy and credibility were populists able to bring regime change. Populists changed constitutions, took over courts, reduced the power of parliaments, concentrated power in the executive, limited the rights to expression and association, and used laws instrumentally to systematically punish critics. Under these conditions they transformed democracies undergoing crises into populist hybrid regimes. They were democratic insofar that they based their legitimacy in the vote and maintained limited civil and political rights. They were simultaneously authoritarian insofar as elections took place under skewed playing fields, rights to expression and association were curtailed, and laws were used against critics.

Postfascism?

After Trump's and Bolsonaro's elections, the term *fascism* returned to civic and academic debates. This is not the first time that the appropriateness of this concept to characterize nondemocratic regimes has been debated. Latin American Marxists argued that the military dictatorships of the 1960s and 1970s were fascist because they were anticommunist and had a middle-class social base, and the monopoly faction of the bourgeoisie was dominant. Some argued that the charismatic leader was replaced by a technocratic civilian-military elite. Sociologist Theotonio Dos Santos (1977: 190) concluded his article by assuring readers, "The threat of fascism is the fundamental political problem in Latin America." In the same issue of *Revista Mexicana de Sociología*, Agustín Cueva (1977) noticed that fascism could assume different forms and that the nations of the Southern Cone – Brazil, Argentina, and Chile – experienced a different type of fascism. Like under classical fascism, monopoly capital was dominant; it was terrorist and anti-working class, and emerged when capitalism was in crisis. Yet this fascism was not the same. It was not nationalist because of Latin America's dependency, and differently from classical fascists, Augusto Pinochet and other military leaders mobilized their middle-class supporters in the streets at the moment of the coup, only to later deactivate them.

The Marxist structuralist theory of fascism that focused on the acute economic crisis of capitalism, on the dominance of monopoly capital, and on the argument that its social base was made up of the petty bourgeoisie has several problems. These interpretations can become ahistorical when all repressive and authoritarian governments are labeled as fascist. Structuralist approaches do not take fascist beliefs into account. Facism's social base cannot be reduced to the middle class because it appeals to all classes. Some also neglected fascist leadership, and as George Mosse (1999: 37) wrote, "discussing the movements without the leaders is rather like describing the body without the soul."

Historians, as argued earlier in this Element, situate fascism in a particular historically bounded constellation of events. Important changes illustrate that what came after fascism is different. First, when former fascists accepted that elections ought to be used to get to power, facism became a different ism that can be described as radical right populism or as postfascism. Second, biological racism was replaced with cultural forms of racism. Culture is understood with essentialist criteria as rooted in the territory, language, and religion of an ethnic group. Each ethnicity, it is argued, has cultural rights, and to try to assimilate people of different cultures is an attack on human diversity. Scholars of the Nouvelle Droite hence propose to stop immigration of ethnic groups who have their own religion, culture, mores, or ways of being. They argue that in the name of multiculturalism global elites seek cheap labor. Therefore, at least theoretically, they do not advocate for the extermination of the essentially culturally different other who ought to stay in the soils where it belongs. Yet what to do with the descendants of immigrants? Are they unassimilable because culture, like biology, is an essence? Third, they do not support similar policies or share similar notions about gender and sexuality. Some, especially in the Americas but also Vox in Spain and Giorgia Meloni in Italy, consider that gender ideology, abortion, same-sex marriage, and LGTBQ+ rights are causing moral decay, lowering white birth rates, replacing natives with non-white immigrants, and destroying the heterosexual nuclear family. Others, like Marine Le Pen, embrace LGTBQ+ and gender rights, arguing that immigrants from Muslim nations aim to impose their traditional morality in states built on notions of *laïcité*. Fourth, differently from the fascist era when the interventionist and strong state was put at the center of economic policies, nowadays the radical populist right-winger or postfascist proposes different roles for the state in the economy. Some European leaders and parties propose to strengthen the welfare state for natives only. Jair Bolsonaro promoted neoliberalism, while Javier Milei was a libertarian. Donald Trump at the same time endorsed neoliberalism at home and restricted free trade and globalization.

Roger Griffin (2020: 205–209) distinguishes three postfascist families: Nazi hot spots, fascist terrorists, and identitarians. The latter emerged in France in

2012 and have sprung up all over Europe and the United States. José Pedro Zúquete (2018: 38, 42) in *The Identitarians* writes that for them "everything is political"; their militancy is a way of life with "the goal of retaking territory and reconquering minds and souls." They argue that the "new class war of the twenty first century, is, and will be, between the people (still territorialized, still attached to traditions) and the globalist (and therefore rootless) elites, as a cosmopolitan hyperclass at the center of a cosmocracy" (Zúquete 2018: 126). In the US, their most common name is the alternative right or simply alt-right. They became well known during Trump's first presidential campaign when Steve Bannon became the executive chairman of the Breitbart News Organization, claiming that it would be "the platform for the alt-right" (Wolff 2018: 138). Democratic candidate Hillary Clinton forcibly denounced Bannon, Breitbart, and the alt-right in these terms:

> This is not conservatism as we have known it. This is not Republicanism as we have known it. These are race-baiting ideas, anti-Muslim and anti-immigrant ideas, anti-woman – all key tenets making up an emerging racist ideology known as the "alt-right" ... The de facto merger between Breitbart and the Trump campaign represents a landmark achievement for the alt-right. A fringe element has effectively taken over the Republican Party. (Green 2017: 213)

Her words were prophetic as an array of alt-right militants, right-wing militias, and believers of conspiracy theories such as QAnon stormed the Capitol Building in an attempt to cleanse it of corrupt, pedophile, and evil politicians and to reinstate their hero, Trump, to office because, they argued, the election was stolen.

Conclusion: Populists, Wannabe Fascists or Postfascists?

Andrea Mammone (2015) wrote that the word *populist* normalizes and sanitizes extremist antidemocratic actors. New terms are perhaps needed to understand the permutations of the radical right when its members stopped accepting electoral results they dislike and promoted violence against enemies constructed as the total other because of their race, ethnicity, religion, or culture. Federico Finchelstein argues that nowadays radical right populists are abandoning populism and becoming wannabe fascists. Like their predecessors, wannabe fascists glorify violence, use racism and xenophobia to construct enemies, replace historical truths with lies, and have switched "from generic rhetoric about the enemy (the elites, traitors, deep state, outsiders, etc.) to the specific naming of racial, political, and/or sexual, and/or religious foes who are then met with political violence" (Finchelstein 2024: 85). However, these leaders are not fascist because they have not descended to terror to get rid of their enemies or to dictatorship – at least not yet. Filchelstein's provocative argument focuses more on the actions and ideologies of leaders, stressing their lack of an uncompromising fascist will that explains why they have remained in the limbo between authoritarian populism and fascism. He also considers historical, structural, and institutional factors that have constrained wannabe fascists from fully following the path of their predecessors.

Enzo Traverso (2019) developed a complementary structuralist interpretation. He argues that to have fascism, a leader is not enough because a mass movement is also required. He proposes that the twenty-first century is a new historical and unstable constellation different from the one that allowed fascists to get to power in the 1920s and 1930s. The character of racism changed from biology to culture, anti-Semitism did not disappear but muted into Islamophobia, and the extreme right accepted features of democracy like elections. Perhaps under this new constellation fascism will remain aspirational. If this is the case, their effects on democracies will be different from classical fascism that ended up replacing it with dictatorship. Wannabe fascists or postfascists, like populists, will probably undermine democracy from within. Geoff Eley (2023: 56) argues that even though classical fascism was a unique historical event, the authoritarian projects of the radical right are similar because, like fascist projects, they aim "to silence and even murder ... opponents rather than arguing with them; prefer an authoritarian state over democracy; [and] pit an aggressively exclusionary idea of the nation against a pluralism that values and prioritizes difference."

The next section focuses on the conditions that allow semi-democratic forces to replace democracy with dictatorship, and the different outcomes of the conflicts between two antagonistic camps under various institutional and structural conditions that could but do not necessarily lead to the slow death of democracy.

5 Fascism, Populism, and Democracy

It was previously noted that fascism and populism are not external viruses that invade and attack democracy from outside, and that they are rather possible outcomes of processes of democratization. Yet their effects are different. There is a consensus that shows how fascists in power abolished civil liberties and pluralism, attempted to control organizations of civil society, and got rid of the open public sphere. There is no such census on populism and democratization. Whereas, for some, populism in power slowly undermines democracy by concentrating power in the presidency and restricting rights of information and association (Weyland 2019), for others, it is the road to democratize political systems that are ruled by technocratic elites on the back of people's sovereignty (de Benoist 2018; Mouffe 2018). Yet defenders of populism differ in the type of populism they advocate. For the left, the people of populism ought to be conceived as the plebs who are exploited and/or marginalized by elites (Mouffe 2018). Right-wing scholars claim that populists are defending the people understood as rooted in territories, immemorial histories, languages, and religions from global elites. They argue that multiculturalism and immigration are destroying the people and the nation (de Benoist 2018: 357). Yet differently from the left that proposes to use the state to reduce inequalities, the right is divided between market-oriented proposals and welfare chauvinists who aim to use the welfare state for nationals only.

I focus on the effects of fascism and populism on democracy, looking at the interactions between two camps in moments when the political is understood as the struggle between friend and enemy. Fascists and populists thrive on polarization and antagonistic confrontation between two camps. Whereas fascists aim to eliminate the other camp using warlike methods, populists do not go as far and try to contain and marginalize but not to kill enemies.

The Fascist End of Democracy

Hitler and Mussolini did not get to power with coups or by winning elections. They were invited by conservative elites to form coalition governments in nations in which the state was weak, unwilling or unable to maintain order due to strong polarization in the streets and political deadlock. Between 1919 and 1922 there were six changes of government in Italy, and in 1919–20, during the *biennio rosso*, the country experienced takeover of private property, including the occupation of factories in Turin in 1920 (Kershaw 2015: 135). The specter of Bolshevism was becoming a real possibility, and fascists were perceived as the only organized group that could use violence and terror to reestablish law and order. The fear of communism also influenced the Catholic Church. Pope Pius XI was convinced that communism was worse than fascism, and he was indifferent to political liberties (Paxton 2005: 108). German soldiers and workers established councils in major cities, and the right responded violently with a coup attempt in 1919 and Hitler's failed Beer Hall Putsch in Bavaria in 1923 (Bermeo 2003: 36). Violence that was "endemic in taverns and gathering spaces of all sorts eventually became the regime's undoing" (36). Six national ballots were held in Germany between May 1928 and November 1932 (38). Italy and Germany experienced the deadlock of constitutional governments "(produced in part by the polarization that the fascists abetted); conservative leaders who felt threatened by the loss of their capacity to keep the population under control at a moment of massive popular mobilization; an advancing Left; and conservative leaders who refused to work with that Left and who felt unable to continue to govern against the Left without further reinforcement" (Paxton 1998: 17).

Having been invited to form coalition governments by King Victor Emmanuel and by Paul von Hindemburg, Mussolini and Hitler outmaneuvered their allies and turned democratic regimes in crisis into dictatorships. Whereas it took three years for Mussolini to control the Italian state and, afterward, to deal with the power of the king, Hitler established his total domination of Germany within six months. After the fire at the Reichstag, Hitler used laws that empowered him to govern by decree for four years. When the laws expired in 1937 Hitler extended them for another five years. Franz Neumann (1944: 52) argues that "the Enabling Act represented the most radical departure from the principles of liberal constitutionalism." All legal protection of speech, assembly, property, and personal liberty were suspended, "permitting authorities to arrest suspected 'terrorists' (i.e. communists) at will, and gave the federal government authority over the state government's police power" (Paxton 2005: 107). Open terror against opponents was the main method of taking control, alongside heavy pressure to comply with the new regime (Kershaw 2015: 214).

In Italy the struggle between Mussolini, his party militants, and the conservative establishment was more gradual. The kidnapping and assassination of socialist leader Giacomo Metteotti by squadrists finally led Mussolini to mobilize the fascist militia so as to abolish parties, civil liberties, and the free press. By early 1927 Italy had become a one-party dictatorship (Paxton 2005: 109–110).

After concentrating power fascists got immersed in a four-way struggle for dominance among "the leader, his party (whose militants clamor for jobs, perquisites, expansionist adventures, and the fulfillment of elements of the early radical program), the regular state functionaries such as police commanders and magistrates, and the traditional elites – churches, the army, the professions, and business leaders" (Paxton, 1998: 18). Despite its constant flux, fascism "left the distribution of property and the economic and social hierarchy largely intact" (Paxton 2005: 141).

Duplication of lines of authority explains the chaotic and shapeless lines of authority in fascism, which was nonetheless concentrated in the leader as the center that mediated or provoked conflicts and divisions to reign supreme. In Italy, for example, "the local party chief flanked the appointed mayor, the regional party secretary flanked the prefect, the Fascist militia flanked the army and so on ... After the Nazi Party attained power, the parallel organizations threatened to usurp the functions of the army, the Foreign office and other agencies" (Paxton 2005: 124–125). The Nazi state fragmented into a normal state that upheld traditional positive legality – meaning citizens could get married or be convicted of murder according to normal law – and a prerogative state that enacted arbitrary rules such as who was a member of the nation-state and who had rights (Müller 2011: 119).

Federico Finchelstein studied the texts of fascist theorists and the declarations of leaders and activists to argue that the fascist dictatorship was not conceived as a temporary event. Rather it was imagined as permanent and personalized in an almost divine leader. Their justification was "that if the leader truly and permanently embodied the people and the nation, there was no need to put the one-man leadership into question" (Finchelstein 2024: 160).

Populisms and the Possible Slow Death of Democracy

Differently from fascists, who were ideologically committed against parliamentary democracy, populists pledged to fight to improve it. However, despite their claims to be real democrats, populists in office, regardless of their ideological self-identification, eroded democracies worldwide in the twenty-first century. Several chapters in the *Routledge Handbook of Global Populism* illustrate patterns of democratic backlash in Asia, Africa, Europe, and the Americas (Filc 2019; Levistsky and Loxton 2019; Lowndes 2019; Mietzner 2019; Resnick 2019; Rivero 2019). When religious-ethnic constructs are used to define the people, the result is that nonbelievers or members of other religions are excluded or targeted as polluting the purity of the people and the national community, as illustrated in Narendra Modi's India, Recep Tayyip Erdoğan's Turkey, Benjamin Netanyahu's Israel, or Donald Trump's United States. Other populists like Thaksin Shinawatra in Thailand, Michael Sata in Zambia, or Hugo Chávez in Venezuela included the politically, economically, and culturally excluded with the condition of their loyalty and transformed political rivals into enemies of the leader and the people.

The question, then, is: Under what conditions are populists able to replace democracy with autocracy? Do populisms lead not only to democratic decline but also to regime change? What are the institutional, economic, and supranational factors that explain democracy's survival or its death?

Political scientist Kurt Weyland (2019) provides the first answer by differentiating two routes by which populists have historically eroded democracy. The first is that, when they closed institutional channels to the opposition, its most reactionary sectors plotted military coups. The history of Latin America from the 1930s to the 1970s oscillated between populists in power and military coups. After the third wave of democratization shaped the international community to accept elections as the only tool to name and remove presidents, coups became more costly (Bermeo 2016). The successful military interventions in Thailand against Thaksin in 2006 and Yingluck Shinawatra in 2014 are the exception and not the rule to displace populists from office. Nowadays, as Weyland and others argue, populism often leads to slow democratic erosion. Whereas it is relatively easy to point to the events, the dates, and the actions that led to the death of democracy with a fascist coup in Italy after the assassination of Giacomo Matteotti or the Nazis' abolition of democracy with the Enabling Act of 1933, it is more complicated to point out the thresholds when a liberal democracy in crisis becomes a populist hybrid regime (democratic-authoritarian), and when it becomes competitive authoritarian (Peruzzotti 2022).

When populists get to power, they enter confrontations with non-populist parties and associations of civil society, as well as with national and supranational institutions. If populists prevail in these conflicts, they transform democracies in crises into populist hybrid regimes, meaning that populist regimes have democratic and authoritarian characteristics. They are in the democratic camp because elections are used as the only legitimate mechanism to get to office. For free elections to take place, the rule of law protects fundamental rights to information and association or at least ensures that these rights are not severely curtailed. Hybrid regimes simultaneously belong to the authoritarian camp because political rivals are considered existential enemies. Populists claim to represent and to even embody a section of the population while excluding other sectors using ethnic criteria or their position in the social structure, and because a leader is built into the sole authentic and authorized voice of the people. The coexistence of formal democratic rules and autocratic methods "creates[s] an inherent source of instability" (Arato and Cohen 2022: 148). Hybrid regimes either democratize or become fully authoritarian. In what follows, the different aftermaths of the possible confrontations between a populist in office and the non-populist camp are outlined. This differentiation does not imply a teleological argument that populism will inevitably end up in an electoral autocracy; it rather aims to illustrate the indeterminacy of political confrontations between two camps that see each other as enemies.

Political scientist Julio Carrión (2022) uses the term *Hobbesian moment* to analyze the struggles between populists in office versus the non-populist camp in these decisive and uncertain critical junctures. Their confrontations could lead to four different outcomes: (1) successful or failed coup attempts; (2) supranational institutions that tame populists; (3) successful resistance of the non-populist camp (parties, social movements, state bureaucrats who have loyalty to their position and not to a politician) that allows for the survival of a delegitimized democracy; (4) regime change and transformation of the constitution and electoral rules by the winning populist camp.

(1) Persistence of the Military Coup Temptation

Polarization could induce radicalized sectors of the opposition to try a military coup in order to stop the populists – a risky action indeed in a new international constellation that does not favor military takeovers. When coups failed as in Venezuela (2002) or Turkey (2016), the outcomes led to the further radicalization of populist leaders and their projects. After the miscarried coup attempt, Hugo Chávez adopted socialism of the twenty-first century as a new model of direct democracy and of state-led development. The opposition tried a general strike to oust Chávez. Later it used elections to unsuccessfully attempt to replace him. Following Chávez's death, his handpicked successor, Nicolás Maduro, was elected president in 2013 but lost congressional elections to the opposition in 2015. Maduro subsequently ruled by decree, called for a new constitutional assembly to take power away from the opposition-controlled legislature, and used brutal repression. Venezuela is no longer a democracy (López Maya 2018).

As in Venezuela, a coup was used in Turkey to try to get rid of a polarizing president, and its aftermath led to further democratic erosion. This was the first coup attempt that was stopped by citizen's mobilization. Recep Tayyip Erdoğan, the leader of the Justice and Development Party (AKP), won the parliamentary elections of 2002, and since then, AKP has always won at the polls. Erdoğan entered conflicts with two players of the establishment with veto power who wanted to preserve the legacies of the Kemalist secular state: the military and the judiciary. The aftermath of the failed coup of 2016 led to 40,000 arrests and the suspension of "approximately 125,000 military officers, civil servants, judges, prosecutors, police officers, teachers, and academics" (Altinordu 2019: 33). Erdoğan used the state of emergency to rule by decree and to call for a constitutional referendum in 2017 that transformed Turkey's parliamentarism into a presidential system and "to the de facto and de jure rise of a competitive authoritarian regime" (Baykan 2018: 253).

(2) Supranational Institutions

The second possible outcome is that supranational institutions restrain populists. Whereas supranational organizations were not able to control Hugo Chávez, Alexis Tsipras and his party, the Coalition of the Radical Left (Syriza), surrendered to the demands of the International Monetary Fund, the European Central Bank, and the Council of Europe. Tsipras's campaign pledged to resist austerity policies and the demands of foreign creditors. Once in office after winning a referendum, he capitulated to the demands of the Troika in

July 2015. Syriza became a party of the establishment as its radical populist promises evaporated.

(3) Temporary Defeat of the Populist Camp

A third outcome occurs when non-populist parties, social movements and other organizations of civil society, and state officials who see themselves as servants of the the state and not of a politician resist and ultimately overshadow populist proposals of regime change. Donald Trump and Jair Bolsonaro faced the resistance of the judiciary, the legislative, state officials, political parties in the opposition, and mobilized citizens. Trump was constrained by a system of checks and balances and stronger institutions. Polarization "of the two-party system limit[ed] Trump's popular support and guarantee[d] intense opposition" (Weyland 2020: 399). His policies, style, and rhetoric energized the Democratic Party and brought a coalition of all those who were fed up with him. After losing the 2020 election, he was unable to get institutional support for his claims that the election was rigged. He asked his supporters to stop the steal and save democracy on January 6, 2021. America's democracy survived, but polarization has deepened and his loyal followers have lost trust in elections and the institutions that guarantee their fairness. Trump won the 2024 election, promising to strengthen the executive branch and to overhaul federal bureaucracies to get rid of the "deep state."[4]

Similarly, Jair Bolsonaro, who called himself the Trump of the Tropics, "tested the fabric of Brazilian democracy" (Hunter and Power 2023: 137), but in the end democracy prevailed and the military did not give a coup. Bolsonaro was barred from running for office for eight years by Brazil's highest electoral court, yet his movement remains strong.

(4) Populist Hybrid Regimes

A fourth outcome was the establishment of populist hybrid regimes in Venezuela under Chávez, Orbán's Hungary, Erdoğan's Turkey, and Ecuador under Correa. These leaders defeated the opposition that became demoralized and were able to bring piecemeal regime change that resulted in an inflated presidency. Following Nancy Bermeo's (2016: 10) analysis, executive aggrandizement "occurs when elected executives weaken checks on executive power one by one, undertaking a series of institutional changes that hamper the power of opposition forces to challenge executive preferences." According to Kurt Weyland, two sets of institutional and external opportunities need to coincide:

---

[4] www.donaldjtrump.com.

(1) institutional weakness provides "an opening for the populist suffocation of democracy"; (2) external stimuli such as an acute yet resolvable crisis or "a country blessed by huge hydrocarbon windfalls" (Weyland 2020: 390). By institutional weakness Weyland means frameworks that facilitate these transformations, altering electoral rules or constitutions that could be modified easily. Electoral rules that allowed disproportionate majorities to a winner gave Viktor Orbán an opening in Hungary in 2010. A year later his followers approved a new constitution that increased prime ministerial powers and weakened liberal safeguards. Another manifestation of institutional weakness is when violations of institutional rules are common and do not bring sanctions. Chávez and Correa disregarded existing legislation on how to modify the constitutions of their nations. After constituent assemblies drafted new constitutions that were approved in referenda, transitory councils dominated by the populist coalition were formed and tasked to replace electoral authorities, judges, and officials in charge of the institutions of horizontal accountability. They followed their task and replaced independent officers with regime cronies (de la Torre and Ortiz 2016; Hawkins 2016).

External opportunities such as a grave but manageable crisis or mineral commodities windfall permitted these leaders to further increase the power of the executive. Orbán successfully dealt with a deep economic crisis (Weyland 2020: 397). Venezuela and Ecuador were rich in hydrocarbons and reaped huge benefits from the commodity boom of the 2000s that catapulted oil and natural gas prices to record levels.

One can recognize a populist hybrid regime when (1) elections are not free and fully competitive, (2) when freedom of expression and association are systematically curtailed, and (3) when laws are used instrumentally to serve the interests of the incumbent (Arato and Cohen 2022: 136). Democracies polarized by populists could not last for long periods of time because of their view of the political as an existential struggle between two camps where citizens, organizations of civil society, and even bureaucrats have to pick sides. In addition, populist sources of legitimacy are paradoxical: free elections together with views of the people as one and a leader as a savior. At the same time that populists use elections to get to power legitimately, they consider that they and only they should win them since they are the only real representatives of the authentic people. Because the mission of the leader is the people's liberation from oppressive elites, they do not feel constrained by institutions and norms, as these are considered tools of the elites to control the people.

(5) Competitive Authoritarianism

Hybrid regimes could become competitive authoritarian when incumbents control the institutions of horizontal and vertical accountability. Elections under competitive authoritarianism cease to be mechanisms of accountability but become "instead a mechanism of regime reproduction. They serve to legitimize the extraordinary aggrandizement of executive power" (Carrión 2022: 180). Competitive authoritarian regimes do not meet minimal democratic credentials and are forms of electoral autocracy in which "the formal democratic institutions exist and are meaningful, but in which incumbents abuse and skew the playing field to such an extent that the opposition's ability to compete is seriously compromised" (Levitsky and Loxton 2019: 336). Despite the difficulties to defeat incumbents, the opposition tries hard even though it often fails, as in Hungary (2022) or Turkey (2023) (Esen and Gumuscu 2023; Scheppele 2022). But when an incumbent such as Nicolás Maduro in Venezuela tilts the playing field so heavily that he can no longer lose elections, that regime "has become effectively a single party state" despite appeals to popular sovereignty (Arato and Cohen 2022: 151).

Political scientists use the concept of competitive authoritarian regimes to describe Erdoğan's regime after the coup (Baykan 2018), and right- and left-wing populist administrations such as those of Alberto Fujimori, Rafael Correa, Hugo Chávez, and Evo Morales in Latin America (Levitsky and Loxton 2019). This category focuses on the strategies of populists in power and the resulting institutional design. Researchers could use this category to study how populist polarization and the transformation of rivals into enemies could lead to the slow death of democracy. However, competitive authoritarian regimes are not homogeneous (Cameron 2018). Whereas Alberto Fujimori did not mobilize supporters, Hugo Chávez created participatory forms of democracy at the local level and mobilized followers. To correct overgeneralizations of the use of the term, scholars could develop subtypes that differentiate processes of participation, inclusion, and innovation.

Conclusions

Nancy Bermeo (2003: 221) concludes her classic volume *Ordinary People in Extraordinary Times* by demonstrating that political elites were responsible for democracy's demise. In Italy and Germany elites invited fascists to the executive under conditions of polarization in the streets, constitutional deadlock, fear of an imminent communist revolution, their unwillingness to rule in coalition with the moderate left, and their arrogant assumption that they could control fascist leaders. They were outpowered by fascists, yet traditional elites preserved their economic power and social position. History could have had different outcomes if elites did not try to use fascist movements and their leaders to get rid of the left. Political and some economic elites continue to normalize and sanitize radical right populists or wannabe fascists when they invite them to be part of coalition governments, or when they allow them to take over a major conservative party such as the Republican Party in the United States. If elites were the culprits who caused the end of democracy during the interwar period, currently they are allowing reactionary leaders and their movements to erode democracy, or collaborating with them. It is an open question if the military and other elites will follow political, economic, and media elites to allow them to successfully bring about the demise of democracy.

When fascists or populists get to office in polities with constitutional deadlocks, civil confrontations that the state cannot or is unwilling to control, and crises of democratic legitimacy there is the possibility of democratic backsliding, even that the democratic government could eventually be replaced with a dictatorship. But possibility is not the same as inevitability. There is no teleology that leads populism in power inevitably to killing democracy. Most often various governments that are more or less democratic and authoritarian have emerged. The gray area between democracy and autocracy is unstable and governments democratize or become dictatorships. Weyland (2020) correctly focuses on institutional arrangements and external stimuli such as a resolvable crisis or oil and mineral windfalls to explain the few cases when populists were able to bring regime change. Yet even when democracy has survived, populists in office have contributed to further delegitimize its institutions and norms – particularly when they cry fraud if they lose an election, transform rivals into enemies, and raise the stakes of elections as all-or-nothing confrontations.

Fascism is different from populism because it got rid of elections, used widespread internal and external violence, and employed ceremonies of mass assent as instruments of legitimation. For the time being, regardless of whether we call them right-wing populist extremists, wannabe fascists, or postfascists, these leaders, their movements, and their parties will continue to operate in the democratic game while undermining the democratic legitimacy of procedures and institutions. Whether the radical right will be willing and able to get rid of democracy is unknown. Perhaps more democracies will move to the gray area between authoritarianism and full democracies, or perhaps they will incrementally move closer to the autocratic end, becoming "democraduras" (limited political democracies) or "dictablandas" (soft dictatorships) (O'Donnell and Schmitter 1986: 13). It is tempting to share Weyland's optimistic conclusion that only when populists govern under facilitating institutional conditions and externalities do they bring about regime change, and that hence democracy will not collapse in most nations of the world. But the elites' normalization of the radical right (often of fascist origins), the global diffusion of right-wing extremist populism, and the realization that, even when leaders like Trump or Bolsonaro failed as presidents, they continue to have mass bases of supporters who idolize them as redeemers could lead us to more pessimistic conclusions.

6 Conclusions

This Element started with a quote by George Mosse about the need for an accurate analysis of the past in order to speculate about the future. Analytical categories, concepts, definitions, and theories are hence crucial, and that is why this Element discussed epistemological and analytical strategies. At present, and despite the abundance of case studies and theoretical elaborations, there is no consensus on what fascism or populism are or how best to define them. Perhaps we will never reach a definitional consensus because these terms are not just analytical categories that are used by scholars in the ivory tower of academia, but words used in political conflicts. Most pundits use populism to evoke images of irrationality and danger to democracy. Fascism recalls a violent past that led to the genocide of populations racialized as threats to the purity of the people. The use and abuse of these emotionally charged words explain why there are periodic calls to ban them from academic vocabulary, or to keep them as insults against whoever we dislike. Abolitionism, however, does not solve the problem because, despite their ambiguities and semantic inflation, these categories are indispensable to try to make sense of the past and to differentiate it from the present.

To create consensus, minimum definitions that could travel in time and space were proposed. The first step was to locate them in a domain of social reality. Next, to avoid fuzziness, they were contrasted with their opposites. Despite their elegance and parsimoniousness, one-sentence definitions were declared reductionist, considering key elements of fascism or populism as of secondary importance. Griffin did not place violence as definitional of fascism, while Mudde and Rovira Kaltwasser imposed Eurocentric notions that a leader is not central to the definition of populism. In sum they reduced these phenomena to one of their key components. Complex definitions rely on the different aspects of these isms such as ideology, communication style, and organizations highlighted by minimum definitions. Scholars who use complex definitions are not terrorized by fuzziness or gradations and accept the possibility that populism could turn into fascism or vice versa. Yet to be useful for comparative analysis, they need to reduce the number of definitional components; otherwise their definition might apply only to one or two cases. Federico Finchelstein, for example, reduced the long list of traits of fascism listed in his book *From Fascism to Populism* to just four in his volume *The Wannabe Fascists*.

If scholars can't have the same opinion about definitions, perhaps they could agree on what they do and on their practices to differentiate these isms and find similarities. When compared to the logic of liberal democracy that produces what Laclau (2005) names democratic subjects who accept compromise and pluralism and operate within the bounds of existing institutions, populism and fascism are similar because they share a political logic that produces popular subjects whose demands cannot be fulfilled without the rupture of the existing institutional system. Fascism and populism share similar constructions of the people, leadership, and performance of politics as extraordinary moments of change and renewal. The difference between liberal democrats and fascists and populists, then, lies in different understandings of the political as based on compromise, dialogue, pluralism, and incremental change, or as the struggle between friend and enemy and the need to rupture exclusionary institutional arrangements. Populism is a hybrid that shares with democracy the importance of the vote, and with fascism constructs of the political as the antagonistic confrontation between friend and enemy. Populists could be label as light Schmidtian because they do not aim to physically eliminate the internal or external enemy, and instead marginalize it and keep it alive to continue to argue that they are struggling against oligarchical elites who refuse to allow change.

Nor are all populists the same because the left constructs the people as the plebs, and the right uses cultural, racial-ethnic, and religious criteria to build it as an ethnos. Similarly, not all fascists are the same. The extreme biologization of race to construct the people and its enemies was unique to Nazism. Right-wing dictators borrowed fascist policies like corporatism, using violence to deal with enemies, and ideological glorifications of the nation, among others.

Focusing on practices and actions allows us to differentiate when fascists and populists challenge the power of traditional elites, get to office, and try to change the institutional and normative framework of democracy. When out of power they promise real democracy to replace the failures of parliamentarism to represent the people's will and interests. Yet they use different strategies. Whereas fascists use paramilitarism to fight against the left, racial minorities, and "perverts," populist violence is for the most part confined to words and symbolic action. Populists thrive on polarization and often use violence to attack political enemies in public spaces, the symbols of the power of elites like buildings where the media operates, but without fascist paramilitary organizations and tactics.

Their different uses of violence are contextual and organizational. Classical fascists formed paramilitary parties and emerged in contexts where violence was used by the right and the left and the state had lost the capacity or willingness to impose law and order. If the state has a monopoly on violence, extremist groups could be contained. Yet as in the 1920s and 1930s, the radical right is promoting paramilitary violence to stop the left in Brazil and the US.

Mussolini and Hitler were invited to the executive by political elites who thought that they could domesticate their radicalism. Other elites joined in out of fear of communism, but fascists outmaneuvered them while respecting their property and status. Getulio Vargas and António de Oliveira Salazar used fascist movements and parties to consolidate their grip on power, later repressing and expelling them from office while adopting corporatism. Francisco Franco won a civil war, killed and brutally repressed enemies, merged the Fascist Party with other conservative groups, supported without committing to the Axis Powers in the war, and during the Cold War joined the anticommunist camp. To get to office, populists used open elections and some even struggled against electoral fraud. Marginal elites allied with populists against well-established or traditional elites. Nowadays, like in the interwar period, traditional political elites have enabled right-wing radical populists, normalizing them by inviting them to be part of coalition governments or, in the US, by allowing right-wing extremists to take over a major traditional party.

Whereas fascists undermined and eventually got rid of democracy, not all populists want or are allowed to transform democracies in crisis into populist hybrid regimes or, worse, competitive authoritarian regimes. Only under exceptional institutional settings and externalities were Chávez, Correa, Orbán, and Erdoğan able to bring regime change. Transnational institutions or the resistance of civil society, non-populist parties, and state officials outflanked populists in Greece, Brazil, and the US. Therefore, there is no teleology that leads from populism to the death of democracy. Most often populists displace democracies in crisis that already are in the gray area between democracy and dictatorship, bringing them closer to the nondemocratic pole.

Classical fascism emerged in a particular historical milieu produced by the First World War and the Russian Revolution, which resulted in crises of the state and democracy. Fascism had leaders, paramilitary cadres, political parties, organizations, publications, and the support of liberal professionals, intellectuals, students, and mobilized followers in the streets. When fascists accepted elections, renounced paramilitarism, and modified biological differences into cultural racism, a new historical constellation was put in place. For the time being actors, even those Finchelstein names wannabe fascists, claim to be struggling for democracy even though their actions and words are plainly authoritarian. Intellectual defenses of Schmidtian visions of the political such as Chantal Mouffe's (2018) propose to keep the struggle between friend and enemy as an agonistic conflict that does not aim to physically eliminate the other. It is an open question if the confrontation between friend and enemy could be kept within limits, or whether agonistic politics that accept the right of the enemy to exist will mute the antagonistic conflicts that could be resolved only with the elimination of the enemy.

We are experiencing a global reemergence of the radical right with fascist members who are learning from each other, sharing publications, and meeting regularly both formally and informally. An advantage of using the term *wannabe fascists* is to not allow for the normalization of antidemocratic extremists, and to remind citizens that new and different forms of fascism could arise. It is worth remembering that even though the Latin American military dictatorships of the 1970s were not classical fascism, they inherited and built on fascist notions of the total enemy. The military junta in Argentina put subversives in concentration camps, tortured them, and gave their offspring for adoption to military families. Similarly, narratives and images of the ethnic other as an agent of pollution could lead to expelling the other from the nation and, in extreme situations, to genocide and ethnic cleansing.

Flavio Gentile (2022: 14) writes that as long as the radical populist right renounces violence and uses elections to try to legitimately get to office, they are populists who are getting closer to fascism. They remain in the democratic camp also because power is not permanently embodied in a leader, and populists do not abolish democratic uncertainty as they must win elections that in theory could be lost. The contested term *populism* is useful because it refers to a particular political logic that manufactures enemies, uses reason and passions, and aims to bring back the redemptive promises of democracy. Populisms vary according to how they imagine the people, and its effects on democracy are not the same when challenging the power of elites in office or bringing regime change.

Trump, Bolsonaro, and others might be wannabe fascists who are unwilling to take their ideas to its final consequences or, more likely, they are operating under a new international and intellectual milieu that does not accept dictatorship – at least not yet. Our responsibility as citizens is to not enable politicians who promise to restore the greatness of an imaginary nation clean of "perverts," political, and ethnic enemies. We ought to defend and demand the expansion of rights, pluralism, and an open and democratic public sphere. If in the past political elites caused the demise of democracy (Bermeo 2003: 221), citizens cannot allow politicians of traditional right-wing parties to play with fire again, enabling and normalizing radical right populists assuming that they could tame extreme anti-democrats.

References

Allayrdyce, G. (2003). "Generic Fascism: 'An Illusion'?" in A. Kallis, ed., *The Fascism Reader*. London: Routledge, pp. 49–57.

Altınordu, A. (2019). "A Midsummer Night's Coup: Performance and Power in Turkey's 15 July Coup Attempt," in F. Çiçekoğlu and Ö. Turan, eds., *The Dubious Case of a Failed Coup: Militarism, Masculinities, and 15 July in Turkey*. Singapore: Palgrave, pp. 7–41.

Álvarez Junco, J. (1987). "Magia y ética en la retórica política," in J. Álvarez Junco, ed., *Populismo, cuadillaje y discurso demagógico*. Madrid: Centro de Investigaciones Sociológicas, pp. 219–271.

  (1990). *El Emperador del Paralelo: Lerroux y la Demagogia Populista*. Madrid: Alianza Editorial.

Arato, A. (2012). "Lefort, the Philosopher of 1989." *Constellations* 19 (1): 23–29.

  (2015). "Political Theology and Populism," in C. de la Torre, ed., *The Promise and Perils of Populism*. Lexington: Kentucky University Press, pp. 31–59.

Arato, A. and J. L. Cohen. (2022). *Populism and Civil Society: The Challenges to Constitutional Democracy*. Oxford: Oxford University Press.

Arditi, B. (2015). "The People as Representation and Event," in C. de la Torre, ed., *The Promise and Perils of Populism*. Lexington: Kentucky University Press, pp. 91–113.

  (2024). *Is There Such a Thing as Populism? 3 Provocations and 5½ Proposals*. New York: Routledge.

Auyero, J. (2001). *Poor People's Politics*. Durham, NC: Duke University Press.

Avritzer, L. and L. Rennó. (2023). "Populism, the Pandemic, and the Crises of Bolsonarism," in A. Pereira, ed., *Right-Wing Populism in Latin America and Beyond*. New York: Routledge, pp. 245–263.

Baehr, P. (2008). *Caesarism, Charisma and Fate: Historical Sources and Modern Resonances in the Work of Max Weber*. New Brunswick, NJ: Transaction Press.

Baykan, T. S. (2018). *The Justice and Development Party in Turkey: Populism, Personalism, Organization*. Cambridge: Cambridge University Press.

Bejarano, A. M. (2013). "Politicizing Insecurity: Uribe's Instrumental Use of Populism," in C. de la Torre and C. Arnson, eds., *Latin American Populism in the Twenty-First Century*. Baltimore, MD, and Washington, DC: Johns Hopkins University Press and Woodrow Wilson Center Press, pp. 323–351.

Berezin, M. (2019). "Fascism and Populism: Are They Useful Categories for Comparative Sociological Analysis?" *Annual Review of Sociology* 45: 345–361.

Bermeo, N. (2003). *Ordinary People in Extraordinary Times: The Citizenry and the Breakdown of Democracy*. Princeton, NJ: Princeton University Press.

  (2016). "On Democratic Backsliding." *Journal of Democracy* 27 (1): 5–19.

Bernardino-Costa, J. (2023). "Opening Pandora's Box: The Extreme Right and the Resurgence of Racism in Brazil." *Latin American Perspectives* 50 (1): 98–114.

Biglieri, P. and L. Cadahia. (2021). *Seven Essays on Populism*. Cambridge: Polity Press.

Breaugh, M. (2019). "The Plebeian Experience and the Logic of (Radical) Democracy." *Constellations* 26: 581–590.

Brubaker, R. (2020). "Between Nationalism and Civilizationalism: The European Populist Moment in Comparative Perspective." *Ethnic and Racial Studies* 40 (8): 1191–1226.

Butler, J. (2024). *Who Is Afraid of Gender?* New York: Farrar, Straus and Giroux.

Cameron, M. (2018). "Making Sense of Competitive Authoritarianism: Lessons from the Andes." *Latin American Politics and Societies* 60 (2): 1–22.

Carrión, J. (2022). *A Dynamic Theory of Populism in Power: The Andes in Comparative Perspective*. Oxford: Oxford University Press.

Cheresky, I. (2015). *El nuevo rostro de la democracia*. Buenos Aires: Fondo de Cultura Económica de Argentina.

Cohen, J. L. (2019). "Populism and the Politics of Resentment." *Jus Cogens* 1 (1): 5–39.

Cueva, A. (1977). "La cuestión del fascismo." *Revista Mexicana de Sociología* 39 (2): 469–480.

de Benoist, A. (2018). *Democracy and Populism: The Telos Essays*. Candor, NY: Telos Press.

de la Torre, C. (2010). *Populist Seduction in Latin America*, 2nd ed. Athens: Ohio University Press.

  (2015). "Introduction: Power to the People? Populism, Insurrections, Democratization," in C. de la Torre, ed., *The Promise and Perils of Populism*. Lexington: Kentucky University Press, pp. 1–31.

  (2019). "Global Populism: Histories, Trajectories, Problems, and Challenges," in Carlos de la Torre, ed., *The Routledge Handbook of Global Populism*, 1st ed. London: Routledge, pp. 1–28.

  (2022). "Fascism and Populism," in M. Oswald, ed., *The Palgrave Handbook of Populism*. Cham: Palgrave, pp. 166–177.

de la Torre, C. and C. Arnson. (2013). "Introduction: The Evolution of Latin American Populism and the Debates Over Its Meanings," in C. de la Torre and C. Arnson, eds., *Latin American Populism in the Twenty-First Century*. Baltimore, MD, and Washington, DC: Johns Hopkins University Press and Woodrow Wilson Center Press, pp. 1–37.

de la Torre, C. and A. Ortiz. (2016). "Populist Polarization and the Slow Death of Democracy in Ecuador." *Democratization* 23 (2): 221–241.

de la Torre, C. and T. Srisa-nga. (2022). *Global Populisms*. New York: Routledge.

Diehl, P. (2023). "Gender Contradictions in the Democratic Imaginary: The Populist Response," in C. de la Torre and O. Mazzoleni, eds., *Populism and Key Concepts in Social and Political Theory*. Leiden: Brill, pp. 44–67.

(2024). "Rethinking Populism in Complex Terms," in P. Diehl and B. Bargetz, eds., *The Complexity of Populism: New Approaches and Methods*. New York: Routledge, pp. 19–37.

Dos Santos, T. (1977). "Socialismo y fascismo en América Latina hoy." *Revista Mexicana de Sociología* 39 (1): 173–190.

Eatwell, R. (2007). "The Concept and Theory of Charismatic Leadership," in A. C. Pinto, R. Eatwell, and S. U. Larsen, eds., *Charisma and Fascism in Interwar Europe*. London: Routledge, pp. 1–18.

(2017). "Populism and Fascism," in C. Rovira Kaltwasser, P. Taggart, P. Ochoa Espejo, and P. Ostiguy, eds., *The Oxford Handbook of Populism*. Oxford: Oxford University Press, pp. 363–384.

Elley, G. (2013). *Nazism as Fascism*. New York: Routledge.

(2023). "Liberalism in Crisis: What Is Fascism and Where Does It Come From?" in G. D. Rosenfeld and J. Ward, eds., *Fascism in America: Past and Present*. Cambridge: Cambridge University Press, pp. 45–78.

Esen, B. and S. Gumuscu. (2023). "How Erdoğan's Populism Won Again." *Journal of Democracy* 34 (3): 21–32. https://doi.org/10.1353/jod.2023.a900430.

Filc, D. (2019). "Populism in the Middle East," in C. de la Torre, ed., *The Routledge Handbook of Global Populism*. New York: Routledge, pp. 385–401.

Finchelstein, F. (2014). *The Ideological Origins of the Civil War: Fascism, Populism, Dictatorship in Twentieth Century Argentina*. Oxford: Oxford University Press.

(2017). *From Fascism to Populism in History*. Oakland: University of California Press.

(2020). *A Brief History of Fascist Lies*. Oakland: California University Press.

(2024). *The Wannabe Fascists: A Guide to Understanding the Greatest Threat to Democracy*. Berkeley: University of California Press.

Flynn, B. (2013). "Lefort as Phenomenologist of the Political," in M. Plot, ed., *Claude Lefort: Thinker of the Political*. New York: Palgrave Macmillan, pp. 23–34.

Fritzsche, P. (2016). "The Role of 'the People' and the Rise of National Socialism," in J. Abromeit, B. M. Chesterton, G. Marotta, and Y. Norman, eds., *Transformations of Populism in Europe and the Americas: History and Recent Tendencies*. London: Bloomsbury, pp. 5–15.

Furedi, F. (2018). *Populism and the European Culture Wars: The Conflict of Values between Hungary and the EU*. London: Routledge Apple Books.

Gerbaudo, P. (2019). *The Digital Party: Political Organization and Online Democracy*. London: Pluto Press.

Gentile, E. (2006). *Politics as Religion*. Princeton, NJ: Princeton University Press.

(2008). "Fascism and the Italian Road to Totalitarianism." *Constellations* 15 (3): 291–302.

Gentile, F. (2024). "De Vargas a Bolsonaro: O Brasil como 'laboratorio' ideológico-político para una historia global do populismo." *Lusotopie* 21 (2): 1–21.

Germani, G. (1967). "Mass Society, Social Class, and the Emergence of Fascism." *Studies in Comparative International Development* 3: 189–199. https://doi.org/10.1007/BF02800590.

(1978). *Authoritarianism, Fascism, and National Populism*. New Brunswick, NJ: Transaction Press.

González Trejo, M. (2018). Pueblo y democracia e el populismo venezolano. Unpublished PhD dissertation, Universidad Autónoma de Madrid. https://dialnet.unirioja.es/servlet/tesis?codigo=150228.

Green, J. (2017). *Devil's Bargain: Steve Bannon, Donald Trump, and the Storming of the Presidency*. New York: Penguin Press.

Griffin, R. (2008). *A Fascist Century: Essays by Roger Griffin*. New York: Palgrave.

(2020). *Fascism: A Quick Immersion*. New York: Tibidabo.

Hawkins K. (2016). "Responding to Radical Populism: Chavism in Venezuela." *Democratization* 23 (2): 242–262.

Hawkins, K. and C. Rovira Kaltwasser. (2017). "The Ideational Approach to Populism." *Latin American Research Review* 52 (4): 512–528.

Hennessy, A. (1976). "Fascism and Populism in Latin America," in W. Laqueur, ed., *Fascism: A Reader's Guide. Analysis, Interpretations, Bibliography*. Berkeley: University of California Press, pp. 255–294.

Hochschild, A. R. (2016). *Strangers in Their Own Land: A Journey to the Heart of Our Political Divide*. New York: The New Press.
Hunter, W. and T. J. Power. (2023). "Lula's Second Act." *Journal of Democracy* 34 (1): 126–140.
Jones, L. E. (2016). "Germany's Conservative Elites and the Problem of Political Mobilization in the Weimar Republic," in J. Abromeit, B. M. Chesterton, G. Marotta, and Y. Norman, eds., *Transformations of Populism in Europe and the Americas: History and Recent Tendencies*. London: Bloomsbury, pp. 32–48.
Kallis, A. (2003). "Introduction: Fascism in Historiography," in A. Kallis, ed., *The Fascism Reader*. London: Routledge, pp. 1–43.
Kalyvas, A. (2019). "Democracy and the Poor: Prolegomena to a Radical Theory of Democracy." *Constellations*. 26 (4): 538–553. https://doi.org/10.1111/1467-8675.12451.
Kampwirth, K. (2010). "Introduction," in K. Kampwirth, ed., *Gender and Populism in Latin America*. University Park: University of Pennsylvania Press, 1–25.
Kershaw, I. (2015). *To Hell and Back: Europe 1914–1949*. London. Penguin.
Laclau, E. 1977. *Politics and Ideology in Marxist Theory*. London: Verso.
  (2005). *On Populist Reason*. London: Verso.
Lefort, C. (1986). *The Political Forms of Modern Society: Bureaucracy, Democracy, Totalitarianism*. Cambridge, MA: MIT Press.
Levitsky, S. and J. Loxton. (2019). "Populism and Competitive Authoritarianism in Latin America," in C. de la Torre, ed., *The Routledge Handbook of Global Populism*. New York: Routledge, pp. 334–351.
Levitsky, S. and D. Ziblat. (2018). *How Democracies Die*. New York: Crown.
López Maya, M. (2018). "Populism, 21st-Century Socialism and Corruption in Venezuela." *Thesis 11* 149 (1): 67–83.
Lowndes, J. (2005). "From Founding Violence to Political Hegemony: The Conservative Populism of George Wallace," in F. Panizza, ed., *Populism and the Mirror of Democracy*. London: Verso, pp. 144–172.
  (2019). "Populism and Race in the United States from George Wallace to Donald Trump," in Carlos de la Torre, ed., *The Routledge Handbook of Global Populism*. New York: Routledge, pp. 190–201.
Mammone, A. (2015). *Transnational Neofascism in France and Italy*. Cambridge: Cambridge University Press.
Manin, B. (1997). *The Principles of Representative Government*. Cambridge: Cambridge University Press.
Mann, Michael. (2004). *Fascists*. Cambridge: Cambridge University Press.

McClintock, C. (2013). "Populism in Peru: From APRA to Ollanta Humala," in C. de la Torre and C. Arnson, eds., *Latin American Populism in the Twenty-First Century*. Baltimore, MD, and Washington, DC: Johns Hopkins University Press and Woodrow Wilson Center Press, pp. 203–239.

Mietzner, M. (2019). "Movement Leaders, Oligarchs, Technocrats and Autocratic Mavericks: Populists in Contemporary Asia," in C. de la Torre, ed., *The Routledge Handbook of Global Populism*. New York: Routledge, pp. 370–384.

Mosse, G. (1999). *The Fascist Revolution: Towards a General Theory of Fascism*. New York: Howard Fertig.

Mouffe, C. (2018). *For a Left Populism*. London: Verso.

Mudde, C. (2004). "The Populist Zeitgeist." *Government and Opposition* 39 (4): 541–563.

  (2019). *The Far Right Today*. Cambridge: Polity Press.

Mudde, C. and C. Rovira Kaltwasser, eds. (2012). *Populism in Europe and the Americas*. Cambridge: Cambridge University Press.

  (2017). *Populism: A Very Short Introduction*. New York: Oxford University Press.

Müller, J. W. (2011). *Contesting Democracy: Political Ideas in Twentieth Century Europe*. New Haven, CT: Yale University Press.

Neumann, F. (1944). *Behemoth: The Structure and Practice of National Socialism*. Chicago, IL: Ivan R Dee.

Ochoa, P. (2015). "Power to Whom? The People between Procedure and Populism," in C. de la Torre, ed., *The Promise and Perils of Populism*. Lexington: Kentucky University Press, pp. 59–91.

O'Donnell, G. and P. Schmitter. (1986). *Transitions from Authoritarian Rule: Tentative Conclusions about Uncertain Democracies*. Baltimore, MD: Johns Hopkins University Press.

Ostiguy, P. (2017). "Populism. A Socio-cultural Approach," in C. Rovira Kaltwasser, P. Taggart, P. Ochoa Espejo, and P. Ostiguy, eds., *The Oxford Handbook of Populism*. Oxford: Oxford University Press, pp. 73–97.

Pappas, T. (2019). *Populism and Liberal Democracy: A Comparative and Theoretical Analysis*. Oxford: Oxford University Press.

  (2023). "Populist Leadership" in Carlos de la Torre and Oscar Mazzoleni, eds., *Populism and Key Concepts in Social and Political Theory*. Leiden: Brill, pp. 178–198.

Parsons, T. (1942) Some sociological aspects of the fascist movements. *Social Forces*, 21 (2): 138–147.

Passmore, K. (2014). *Fascism: A Very Short Introduction*. Oxford: Oxford University Press.

Paxton, R. (1998). "The Five Stages of Fascism." *Journal of Modern History* 70: 1–23.

(2005). *The Anatomy of Fascism*. New York: Vintage Books.

Payne, S. (2007). "Franco, the Spanish Falange, and the Institutionalization of Mission," in A. C. Pinto, R. Eatwell, and S. U. Larsen, eds., *Charisma and Fascism in Interwar Europe*. London: Routledge, pp. 53–63.

Pereira Gonçalves, L. and O. Caldiera Neto. (2022). *Fascism in Brazil: From Integralism to Bolsonarism*. New York: Routledge.

Peruzzotti, E. (2013). "Populism in Democratic Times: Populism, Representative Democracy, and the Debate on Democratic Deepening," in C. de la Torre and C. Arnson, eds., *Latin American Populism in the Twenty-First Century*. Baltimore, MD, and Washington, DC: Johns Hopkins University Press and Woodrow Wilson Center Press, pp. 61–85.

(2022). "Contrasting Modern and Contemporary Populist Regimes: From Democratization to Democratic Hybridization." *Populism* 5 (2): 141–157.

(2023). "Populism and Accountability," in C. de la Torre and O. Mazzoleni, eds., *Populism and Key Concepts in Social and Political Theory*. Leiden: Brill, pp. 44–67.

Pinto, A. C. (1995). *Salazar's Dictatorship and European Fascism: Problems of Interpretation*. New York: SSM-Columbia University Press.

(2007). "'Chaos' and 'Order': Preto, Salazar and Charismatic Appeal in Interwar Portugal," in A. C. Pinto, R. Eatwell, and S. U. Larsen, eds., *Charisma and Fascism in Interwar Europe*. London: Routledge, pp. 65–77.

(2020). *Latin American Dictatorship in the Era of Fascism: The Corporatist Wave*. London: Routledge.

Pinto, A. C. and S. U. Larsen (2007). "Conclusion: Fascism, Dictators and Charisma," in A. C. Pinto, R. Eatwell, and S. U. Larsen, eds., *Charisma and Fascism in Interwar Europe*. London: Routledge, pp. 131–137.

Plotkin, M. (2003). *Mañana es San Perón: A Cultural History of Peron's Argentina*. Wilmington, DE: Scholarly Resources.

Porto, M. (2023). *Mirrors of Whiteness: Media, Middle-Class Resentment, and the Rise of the Far Right in Brazil*. Pittsburgh: University of Pittsburg Press.

Postero, N. (2015). "'El Pueblo Boliviano de Composición Plural': A Look at Plurinational Bolivia," in C. de la Torre, ed., *The Promise and Perils of Populism: Global Perspectives*. Lexington: University Press of Kentucky, pp. 398–431.

Rancière, J. (2000). "Jacques Rancière: Literature, Politics, Aesthetics. Approaches to Democratic Disagreement interviewed by S. Guénoun, J. H. Kavanagh and R. Lapidus. " *SubStance* 29 (2): 3–24.

(2010). *Dissensus. On Politics and Aesthetics*. London: Continuum.

Resnick, D. (2019). "The Influence of Populist Leaders on African Democracy," in C. de la Torre, ed., *The Routledge Handbook of Global Populism*. New York: Routledge, pp. 267–281.

Rivero, A. (2019). "Populism and Democracy in Europe," in C. de la Torre, ed., *The Routledge Handbook of Global Populism*. New York: Routledge, pp. 281–294.

Roberts, K. (2023). "Populism and Social Class: Constituting 'the People' and Cleaving the Political Field," in C. de la Torre and O. Mazzoleni, eds., *Populism and Key Concepts in Social and Political Theory*. Leiden: Brill, pp. 67–91.

Rovira Kaltwasser, C. (2019). "La (sobre)adaptación programática de la derecha chilena y la irrupción de la derecha populista radical." *Colombia Internacional* (99): 29–61. https://doi.org/10.7440/colombiaint99.2019.02.

Santos, G. G. da C. (2021). "Anti-gender Politics and the Authoritarian Turn in Brazil." *Brasiliana Journal of Brazilean Studies* 10 (1): 96–124.

Scheppele, K. L. (2022). "How Viktor Orbán Wins." *Journal of Democracy*, 33 (3): 45–61.

Snyder, T. (2017). *On Tyranny: Twenty Lessons from the Twentieth Century*. New York: Tim Duggan Books.

Traverso, E. (2003). *The Origins of Nazi Violence*. New York: New Press.

(2016). *Fire and Blood: The European Civil War 1914–45*. London: Verso.

(2019). *The New Faces of Fascism: Populism and the Far Right*. London: Verso.

(2021). *Las nuevas caras de la derecha*. Buenos Aires: Siglo XXI.

Weber, M. (1978). *Economy and Society*, edited by Guenther Roth and Claus Wittich. Berkeley: University of California Press.

Weyland, K. (2001). "Clarifying a Contested Concept." *Comparative Politics* 34 (1): 1–22.

(2017). "Populism: A Political Strategic Approach," in C. Rovira Kaltwasser, P. Taggart, P. Ochoa Espejo, and P. Ostiguy, eds., *The Oxford Handbook of Populism*. Oxford: Oxford University Press, pp. 48–73.

(2019a). "Populist Authoritarianism," in C. de la Torre, ed., *The Routledge Handbook of Global Populism*. New York: Routledge, pp. 319–334.

(2019b). "Fascism's Missionary Ideology and the Autocratic Wave of the Interwar Years," in André Bank and Kurt Weyland, eds., *Authoritarian Diffusion and Cooperation: The Impact of Interests and Ideology*. New York: Routledge, pp. 19–37.

(2020) "Populism's Threat to Democracy: Comparative Lessons for the United States." *Perspectives on Politics* 18 (2): 389–406.

Wolf, S. (2021). "A Populist President Tests El Salvador Democracy." *Current History* February: 64–70.

Wolff, M. (2018). *Fire and Fury: Inside the Trump White House*. New York: Henry Holt and Company.

Zanatta, L. 2011. *Eva Perón: Una Biografía Política*. Buenos Aires: Sudamericana.

Zúquete, J. P. (2007). *Missionary Politics in Contemporary Europe*. Syracuse, NY: Syracuse University Press.

(2008). "The Missionary Politics of Hugo Chavez." *Latin American Politics and Society* 50 (1): 91–122.

(2018). *The Identitarians: The Movement against Globalism and Islam in Europe*. Notre Dame, IN: Notre Dame University Press.

Acknowledgments

I am grateful to António Pinto and Federico Finchelstein for their invitation to write in their series Elements in the History and Politics of Fascism, and to colleagues and students for their comments. I also want to thank Oscar Mazzoleni and the two anonymous reviewers for their observations on a first draft.

The History and Politics of Fascism

Series Editors
Federico Finchelstein
The New School for Social Research
Federico Finchelstein is Professor of History at the New School for Social Research and Eugene Lang College in New York City. He is an expert on fascism, populism, and dictatorship. His previous books include *From Fascism to Populism in History* and *A Brief History of Fascist Lies*.

António Costa Pinto
University of Lisbon
António Costa Pinto is a Research Professor at the Institute of Social Sciences, University of Lisbon. He is a specialist in fascism, authoritarian politics, and political elites. He is the author and editor of multiple books on fascism, including (with Federico Finchelstein) *Authoritarianism and Corporatism in Europe and Latin America*.

Advisory Board
Giulia Albanese, *University of Padova*
Mabel Berezin, *Cornell University*
Maggie Clinton, *Middlebury College*
Sandra McGee Deutsch, *University of Texas, El Paso*
Aristotle Kallis, *Keele University*
Sven Reichardt, *University of Konstanz*
Angelo Ventrone, *University of Macerata*

About the Series
Cambridge Elements in the History and Politics of Fascism is a series that provides a platform for cutting-edge comparative research in the field of fascism studies. With a broad theoretical, empirical, geographic, and temporal scope, it will cover all regions of the world, and most importantly, search for new and innovative perspectives.

Cambridge Elements⁼

The History and Politics of Fascism

Elements in the Series

Populism and Fascism
Carlos de la Torre

A full series listing is available at: www.cambridge.org/CEHF

For EU product safety concerns, contact us at Calle de José Abascal, 56–1°, 28003 Madrid, Spain or eugpsr@cambridge.org.

www.ingramcontent.com/pod-product-compliance
Ingram Content Group UK Ltd.
Pitfield, Milton Keynes, MK11 3LW, UK
UKHW022244220326
469255UK00019B/350